"To his family, friends and colleagues, John Lajoie sometimes seems larger than life. Which makes it all the more appropriate that John, in his new book *Trials and Tribulations of a Real Life Private Eye*, is the one PI who puts to rest the myths that surround the profession. John is a real life investigator and the stories in his book are real life case studies. John uses the cases to illustrate the everyday world of private investigators, who are real life business men and women that have families, pay taxes, meet payroll, participate in community and civic affairs, and sometimes deal with pretty strange people and events. Lajoie pulls no punches, spares no one that which they deserve, shares credit with his colleagues, and brings more than a few surprises to the table. Whether you're in the business or not, this is an entertaining and enlightening read."

Don C. Johnson, CLI, CII, Editor, *PI Magazine, Journal of Professional Investigators*

Trials and Tribulations of a Real Life Private Eye

by

John M. Lajoie

authorHOUSE™

1663 Liberty Drive, Suite 200
Bloomington, Indiana 47403
(800) 839-8640
www.AuthorHouse.com

First published by AuthorHouse 08/03/05

ISBN: 1-4208-6939-6 (sc)

Library of Congress Control Number: 2005905937

Printed in the United States of America
Bloomington, Indiana

This book is printed on acid-free paper.

Artistic Coordinator: Mark Waitkus
Illustration: John Gaston
Cover Design: Anne Ashley

DEDICATION

To my wife
Susan J. Lajoie
For putting up with me for all these years and for much, much more.

To my son
Jason M. Lajoie
For figuring out in eighteen years what it took me to figure out in forty six.

To my daughter
Jessica L. Lajoie
For being me in so many ways and loving me anyway.

To my daughter
Jacqueline R. Lajoie
For keeping me young, on my toes, and on the edge.

You are, without question, my heroes and I dedicate this book to all of you.

Honorable Mentions

Abraham Lincoln
For using and realizing the value of a competent PI.

Allan Pinkerton
The first American PI. He saved the life of Abraham Lincoln in 1861.

CONTENTS

Sometimes you have to go on when you don't feel like it, and sometimes you're doing good work when it feels like all you're managing is to shovel shit from a sitting position.

Stephen King

FOREWORD

Trials & Tribulations of a Real Life Private Eye is about real life private investigation. If you're a seasoned private investigator, you'll relate to this book. If you're a newbie PI, you'll learn from it. If you're a wannabe, the book has value. **If you're not a PI, I want you to pretend to be one while reading it.** I think you can manage to daydream. I know you can, especially if you're a lover of PI and detective fiction writings for enjoyment. And who hasn't read these at least once in their life -- I read the *Hardy Boys* series when I was a kid and my wife read *Nancy Drew* books. I wanted to be Frank Hardy. I turned out to be John Lajoie.

The great thing about Frank and Joe Hardy and Nancy Drew is they *never* killed anyone. Unlike some others that come to mind - *Mike Hammer,* for instance. Although I recognize the extraordinary talent and contributions of Mickey Spillane as a writer (a *very* rich writer), I loath the perception he has created about my profession, and I'm here to set the record straight. There are no Mike Hammers out there! Thank God it's fiction. And while I love fiction, I want to make sure the kind that

Hammer represents doesn't distort the public's view of my profession.

Based on the comments I've heard during my life, it seems many people have at least considered at some point what it would be like to be a real life private eye. I hear a lot of affirmations like "I'd love to be a PI" or "I'd make a great PI" or "people say I'd be a great PI." Well, now is your chance to be one, a *real* one, at least for a while. In the pages to come, you'll see the reality separated from the myth. You'll be in my shoes. I tell it like it is, at least through the trials and tribulations of my own experiences, and offer the comments and suggestions that all those experiences have produced. If you take them seriously, they could save you some time and heartache finding your way in the business. And if you're not interested in pursuing the business, they should at least make for good reading.

Contrary to what I know to be absolute mythical belief, not many people have what it takes to be a "great PI" or even a good one. In reality, there are few great PI's, but a lot of good people who are competent investigators. And then there are many more who shouldn't be in the business of investigation, period! In this business, a PI is either competent or incompetent. There really is no middle ground. Very few are in the untouchable league – the "great PI." Most ordinary people form their opinion about what it's like to be a PI from what they've read in fiction novels and newspapers, and what they've seen on television and in the movies. Stories in the movies, on TV, and in fiction novels about PI's are just that: fiction. Or if they're not all fiction, it's never the real or full story. It certainly gives life to the old adage "don't believe everything you read in the newspaper." And you can no doubt extend the adage to fiction novels, television and the movies.

Trials & Tribulations of a Real Life Private Eye is non-fiction writing.

INTRODUCTION

To understand *Trials &Tribulations of a Real Life Private Eye*, you should understand me. You should understand where I came from, how I grew and moved through my childhood into my teen years, how I evolved from a teen to a man, from a man lost to a man found, and from a neophyte private eye to a nationally known and respected professional private investigator. I didn't do it alone. No one does!

When I was a little kid living on Belmont Hill in Worcester, Massachusetts, I did some stupid things. Of course, we all do stupid things from time to time. You just hope and pray the stupidity doesn't kill you.

Bottom line is I was into everything. If it was in the house, I found out about it. If it was locked, I'd find a way to unlock it. If it was up high, I'd manage to find some way to get it. Nothing could be hidden where I couldn't find it. Explore and *investigate.*

The first couple of years after my sister Lisa was born were great because I was no longer the center of attention. I was two and a half when she was born. It was as if I was set free. Mom had a little girl to ga-ga, goo-goo over. That meant independence. My dad was working sixteen hours a day. And that was just fine by me. At three, I was the man of the house while he was away, even if my mother refused to acknowledge it. So from age three to five, I was my own boss...sort of. I did what I wanted, or at least what I could get away with.

I can recall sneaking out of the house before dawn a number of times. It got to be a frequent occurrence so my parents put double locks on the doors; but I still found a way out. I wandered the streets of Belmont Hill looking for nothing in particular. Exploring and *investigating,* I guess. I was rescued either by mom, dad, or Nick Perrone, the upstairs neighbor. Every so often, Nick would catch me out wandering the streets at six in the morning. I was three or four years old. What in the hell was I thinkin'? Starting work a little bit early I'd say...explore and *investigate.* Finally, we moved to Windsor Street and the locks on the doors were not kind to me. To this day, my mother tells people "He liked to escape." It's probably a good thing I've never been locked up.

The stupidity continued on Windsor Street even though I was older. I hooked up with this kid the same age as me named John Lynch. He was my best friend during my early years; that is, until we nailed a kid to a cross and egged him. I think tomatoes might have been part of it as well. But it really didn't happen the way you might think. Lynchie and I ambushed and tied this neighborhood bully to a cross one day. We were sick of this kid and we wanted him to pay for his sins. I could name him but I won't. The crime scene was in an exposed area underneath the first floor of a rest home on Uxbridge Street. We beat him up but we were not without mercy; we let him live. He deserved it as far as we were concerned. No more bully stuff. No more threats. Life would be peaceful from here on out. Wrong! The bully's brother and friends showed up at my door. The parents of the bully wanted blood.

So did my father. The result was a lengthy lashing with what my father called "the nine ends," a rather frightful, homemade, behavior modification tool. I'm not about to describe it; use your imagination. I'd say it worked real well. I got lashed with it more than a few times for deeds unbecoming. My mother never interfered because every so often she'd dish out her own form of corporal punishment. It was the way it worked back then. Nobody complained because it was medicine. The threat of "the nine ends" did it for me; it was a great deterrent. Ma's punishments were ice cream and cake compared to "the nine ends," but I always let her think what she doled out was much worse than it actually was because she was the sympathizer. Dad really didn't give a shit what I thought when it was time for punishment. Sympathy was not his thing when I needed a good lesson. Discipline – I hated it then but I'm thankful now. It has kept me in check during exploration and *investigation.*

While on Windsor Street, I garnered friendships that last to this day. People were good to my parents and me, people like Althea (Al) and Paul Trottier, Kathy and Norman (Buster) Dion, and Jimmie Barbato. I played with their kids and became their friends. I hung with John Lynch, Gary Trottier and his little brother Brian, Greg Kazarian, Jim Roberts, Mike Kostaras, Mary Costello, Christine Howe, Jimmy Rovezi, Fred Stout, Luis Rivera, Rick Sargent, and sometimes his younger brother Steve who is now a Captain on the Worcester Police Department. Over the years, we've worked opposite sides on a few criminal cases and he's always been courteous and honorable. I have great respect for Steve Sargent; he's a good investigator but a better man. I predict he'll be a Chief someday. I had puppy love crushes on Donna Quinn, Linda Flynn, Katie Gallant, and Robin Sargentelli. The crush on Donna was mutual, but I doubt the others knew until now. It was a great melting pot in a blue collar neighborhood. Whiffle and punch ball was *big.* The Red Sox were heroes; 1967 broke our hearts. I was nine years old. Thirty seven years later, I watched every pitch to victory. My son was at the Red Sox World Series parade in Boston in 2004. I'd have killed to go to a World Series parade in 1967 with my friends. But it was not to be. Instead, we clung to hope and bragged who could hit the most home runs at Trottier's whiffle ball field. We attended Harlow Street Elementary School and St. Bernard's Church. Father Needham was revered. Principal Lennon was feared. We watched in horror as JFK, RFK and MLK were assassinated. Life went on. We listened to The Beatles on the radio. We held the neighborhood together with hope, friendship, and teamwork. There can be no doubt we always worked as a team. It is here where I learned the great lesson of "never forget where you come from." It holds me together today as it did yesterday, and the day before. And all the way back to 1963. Believe it or not, it helps hold Lajoie Investigations, Inc. (LII) together today. Just ask any of the people who work there. The value of teamwork is priceless.

Windsor Street ushered in two more sisters in Lori and Lynn. The family was complete: Raymond (Mondo) Lajoie; Coralie (CoCo) Lajoie; John; Lisa; Lori; and Lynn. There are nine years between the oldest and the youngest. Lori Ann Lajoie is now deceased having succumbed to the painful experience of ovarian cancer in 2001. I was there when she took her last breath of hospital air. *Thirty seven years old.* Life is precious. You learn to treasure life after an experience like that; Lajoie Investigations didn't seem at all important when it was happening. *Investigation* was the furthest thing from my mind.

In July of 1971, we moved to the 'burbs. Dad had been named head golf professional at the Worcester Country

Club (WCC). He deserved it. It was exciting. New Job. New house. New school. New friends. Wow! West Boylston, Massachusetts; only about five miles from the old neighborhood. Great place.

Then why did I feel terrible? I really didn't want to go, but what choice did I have? I left my friends behind. Although I didn't feel too good about it, I managed to get over my heartache. I left the old neighborhood in body but not in mind and spirit. It was about this time when I decided to play some serious golf. It was a decision that would eventually aid in the start of my investigation agency.

Almost immediately, I made new friends and lots of them. Kenny Bryant, Brian Buchyn, Dave Dylewicz, John Handy, Dave Moorefield, Pete Farnsworth, Joe Evangelista, Mark Lavoie, Karen Metcalf, Lisa Naylor, Judy Hehir, and many others. West Boylston High School (WBHS) was great...I started to become popular which was scary. I fell in love with Elise Cantillon, but never had the guts to come right out and tell her. I'm sure she knew. Elise moved. I was devastated.

I immersed myself in golf and drastically improved my golf game. My dad was ecstatic. I managed to make a name for myself. From freshman to senior year at WBHS, I was the number one player on the varsity golf team. I started to compete and win tournaments. Coach Bill Foley was a big part of it. My father was pushing me to practice, almost forcing me. I had tremendous ability with a golf club back then. I only recall losing one match in high school competition (Rick Watrous of St. John's High School beat me in a close match). It was a record that probably still stands today at WBHS, but no one was keeping track back then - including me. I advanced to the finals of the state Massachusetts Golf Association Junior-Junior Championship, losing to Randy Millen. I competed at every state and regional amateur level. But I was unable to win the important ones. I could not bring home the top prize in the big tournaments. I was having much too much fun partying and spending lots of time with my girlfriend, Theresa Orne. And I didn't want to sacrifice my social or love life for anything, including golf. I never seriously practiced or dedicated enough time and energy to the game of golf to move to the next level. It's a good thing now that I look back on it because I might not have enlisted in the military right out of high school, which was one of the best decisions I ever made.

I was working at Worcester Country Club during the high school summers, first as a caddie, then in the pro shop, and finally in clubhouse services when I was seventeen. I made a ton of friends and connections at WCC with employees and members. Certainly the most important was the acquaintance I made with Attorney Larry O'Connor; I'll talk about him later. I also worked in the pro shop with a number of people including Timothy Bibaud (Beebs), who is now a Worcester County Assistant District Attorney for head honcho John Conte. I wouldn't be too surprised if Tim Bibaud becomes the Worcester County District Attorney in the not-too-distant future. We had a lot of good times, including a couple of nutso, crazed experiences – one playing four holes of golf in hurricane *Belle* with B. Gardner. The other involved a golf cart. It's one of those stories for another day.

It was tough being the golf pro's son and working at WCC, but I managed. I was treated no different than any other person. My father made sure of it and I was relieved. But he was tough on me and I was difficult to handle, so our relationship was stressed at times during the high school years. I was a teenage boy trying to find my identity. Yet I wasn't paying attention to where I was going in life. I could've cared less at the time. I had an unconcerned, indifferent attitude. I was living for the day. My father was trying to be my father and I wouldn't let him assert his influence over me. Sound familiar?

My mother had her hands full at home. My sister Lori (who I nicknamed Belle) was mentally challenged and remained at home throughout my high school years. The atmosphere was tough on my sister Lisa and my mom because they were Lori's caretakers. I helped out with Lori at times, but my sister Lynn and I each had our own little world. We identified with each other although we were nine years apart. We still do. We're so much alike, yet different. Today we both work long and hard; always have. When we play, we play hard. We both have a witty sense of humor, although Lynn is far more comical than I am. She's a classic impressionist; she does me so well it's scary. When Lynn and I are together laughter fills the air. Laughter reduces life's stresses and makes people smile. We both use our wit and sense of humor at work as well. At Lajoie Investigations, laughter is encouraged. I even tried to make it mandatory. Given the nature of the work, if you do not laugh you *will* cry. And you'll find out why as you read on.

I was an average high school student getting B's and C's without much effort. My SAT scores were average. I was an average kind of guy who never studied much. My mother is not shy to remind me of what I might have done had I applied myself, mustered even a scintilla of effort, and studied. I was on easy street in high school. The last few months of high school are a mystery, a blur. The parties were endless. I did make it through the year, although there were times I thought I wouldn't. I managed to graduate from West Boylston High School in June of 1976. After the post graduation parties, I woke up one morning and wondered what in the hell I was going to do with the rest of my life. I was scared. I had no plan.

I do not recall a college discussion with my parents. Or if there was one, it probably went something like this: "I'm not going to college." What a mistake, but I didn't think so at the time. Among intermittent periods of lucidity, there were relapses of stupidity and this was no exception. I knew I had to do something so I decided to check out the United States Air Force (USAF). I knew I needed a kick in the ass. I knew I needed discipline- there was only so much discipline "the nine ends" could command. And I knew I needed to be able to stand on my own two feet. It was a perfect fit.

In October of 1976, I enlisted in the USAF and headed to San Antonio, Texas for basic training. Easy Street was history. I got knocked down more than a few times. The mind games were endless, but served a purpose. I can still hear Drill Sergeant Butler as if it was yesterday, "Are you out of your freakin' military mind son?" Now there's a man that was out of his mind, but I didn't dare question him. I did everything I was told to do. And I actually loved it. I was sent to Chanute, Illinois for technical training to learn to be a Fuel Systems Technician. After six months of training, I was assigned a permanent duty station in the Civil Engineering Squadron at Little Rock AFB, Little Rock, Arkansas. I had a blast at this base for three years. And Little Rock was a rockin' town in the late 1970's. I turned twenty one in that town- what a night! On the base, I had civilian bosses who were great people and good managers in Marion "Robbie" Robinson and John Gray. John Gray taught me how to work effectively and how to manage time. He was good at it. His work ethic was second to none and he had fun while he was doing it. It rubbed off on me. I was assigned to the PRIME BEEF team (Base Engineer Emergency Force) where teamwork and esprit de corps were paramount. I learned how to work with honor and integrity and be successful at it.

My adult character was forming. I received the Good Conduct Medal. Honor, integrity, and character would one day be requisite for obtaining a Private Detective license in Massachusetts and for its renewal each year. I sure knew the meaning of honor, integrity, and character because I was living it in the USAF.

In October of 1980, my USAF contract was scheduled to expire and I was due for discharge. It was the summer of 1979. I studied and tested for Staff Sergeant (E-5) and made it on the first try which was rare. I was thinking about college. Having a long term relationship with a female was not on my radar screen. My relationship with my high school sweetheart had fallen apart. I was dating a number of women. I went home on leave in August of 1979. On Thursday, August 16, 1979, I met my future wife, Susan J. Pettersen, at the Lori Lajoie Charity Golf Tournament at Worcester Country Club. I knew it right away – there is such a thing as love at first sight. I had to return to Little Rock the next day so we had no chance to date. It would have to wait. Within six months, I received orders to RAF Mildenhall in England. Who could turn down an assignment to Europe, especially England? Not me. Not anyone in their right mind! So I extended my USAF contract for eighteen months and went home in March of 1980 for an extended leave before heading to England. The first thing I did was to find Susan and ask her to dinner. We spent the next twenty five days together. It turned into twenty five years, and we're still counting. Who says long distance relationships can't work out?

I was beginning to find myself and mold my own identity, yet I had no idea I was going to eventually become a PI. Susan was in college and I decided I needed to get a degree as well. Long range plans called for college classes through the University of Maryland while I was in England. I started college in England and completed my freshman year. I had left the game of golf while at Little Rock AFB, but found it again at RAF Mildenhall. My game got stronger in England. I was invited to play on the USAF Command Base Golf Team. What an honor. I played golf with Third Air Force Commander, General John Baxter, and other base dignitaries. I was learning to interact and deal with all kinds of people with differing personality traits. I lived off the base in the small town of Burwell, England, about seven miles from Cambridge and seventy miles north of London. I spent a lot of weekends in Cambridge with friends or traveling to London to explore and *investigate.* I loved going to Speakers Corner, Buckingham Palace, Westminster Abbey, St. Paul's Cathedral, Soho, Liverpool Station, Trafalgar Square, and the colleges and parks of Cambridge to explore and *investigate....* From time to time I even found myself at Dirty Dick's Pub - what a place! Susan came over twice. Romance in England was wonderful. We got engaged.

I discharged from the USAF in March of 1982 and returned home. My parents let me live with them. I felt out of place for the first time in my life. It was as if I was living in the past. I needed an adjustment period. I became a little lost. I was a man without an occupation. I knew I had to complete school so I enrolled full time at Worcester State College. I found work as a full time Security Guard for First Security Services Corp. at Data General Corporation and Astra Pharmaceutical. I got a little taste of *investigation* with First Security but not much. I did rounds, access control, and materials processing. Between work and school, it was sixteen-hour days for almost three years except for college vacations and summers. I still didn't know what career path I'd find. I thought I might want to be an attorney so I researched it and decided to major in history and minor in political science and philosophy. I set my course, full speed ahead. I was still a bit unsure of myself.

The one thing I was certain about, I did something about. I married Susan in June of 1983. We first settled in Boylston. I graduated college in the spring of 1985 and decided to enter the working world instead of law school. We moved to Worcester. Susan was working as a medical technologist in Newton, MA. I started looking for a career job.

Commerce Insurance Company (CIC) of Webster, MA was a new business making a big impact in the property and casualty insurance industry in Massachusetts. They are huge now and employ over two thousand professionals. In 1985, CIC was an upcoming company employing fewer than two hundred. They were looking for college grads to fill a number of attractive positions. I applied and interviewed for one of those positions. I was interested in claims investigation and adjusting. They offered me a job in claims and I accepted. It was a great decision. It was here that I discovered the world of *investigation*! I was trained and put to work in the property department. Within six months I was promoted to the casualty department. Within two years I was promoted to outside casualty investigator/adjuster. I did a year on the road and then moved inside to the Litigation/Other Than Auto Unit working for Karyn MacGillivray.

From 1985 to 1989, I had tremendous opportunity to learn at CIC and I took advantage of it. Explore and *investigate*. But I knew I needed to do my own thing. CIC outsourced investigations to private investigation agencies as did other insurance companies. I was assigning a number of investigations to outside agencies. Paul Peckham from western Massachusetts was the first private eye I ever met. Damn good one too! He let me accompany and observe him on a number of field assignments I outsourced to his company. What an eye-opener. I loved it. Peckham was, and still is, a venerable PI. He first worked for the Poma-Wheeler Agency and then formed his own company called Verified Corporation. Paul did insurance defense investigation, mainly surveillance. At the time, he was the best surveillance investigator out there or so I thought. When I went with him to watch a surveillance unfold, it was eye popping. Paul made it exciting. And he's still at it today, but I'd put Scott Robidoux up against him any day. Scott works for me. Paul trained Scott.

In 1988, I recognized the need for a quality investigative agency in Worcester County. There was no local Worcester private investigation agency getting the job done to my liking, at least none that I saw in my work for CIC. I knew I could do better. I loved investigating and I was good at it. So I set my goal. In June of 1989, I had $11,000 of vested CIC stock in the employee stock ownership program. I did my homework, established a business plan, secured my private detective license, and set out to pursue the American dream. The big deal was to obtain the PI license issued by the Massachusetts Department of Public Safety (now issued by the Massachusetts state police at present). I was nervous about the application process because it seemed tedious, but I had the requisite experience, references, and a clean background. The state requirements also called for a bond and an application fee of $1,100.00 (the highest in the country at the time). That's a *lot* of money. But I came up with it. I had no choice. The application fee has since been cut in half thanks to Phil White, a legendary MA PI who fought with the bureaucrats and pulled off a miracle. After forking out the dough, I got my ticket to ride: the Massachusetts Private Detective License. I was now the "Resident Manager" of Lajoie Investigations, Inc, based in Worcester, Massachusetts.

To say I worked my ass off is an understatement. I hooked up with a criminal defense attorney who taught me the trade. It was time to go. I left a job at CIC paying about $32,000, full benefits, stock program, and plenty of opportunity for advancement. I had a wife making $14.00 per hour. My first born, Jason, was two and a half years old and Susan was about to give birth to Jessica. We had just purchased a house. There were two car mortgages. Talk about pressure!

Explore and *investigate.* What follows are the *Trials and Tribulations of a Real Life Private Eye.*

1
DANGER

We better know there is a fire when we see much smoke rising than we could know it by one or two witnesses swearing to it. The witnesses may commit perjury but the smoke cannot.

Abraham Lincoln

"Danger Will Robinson! Danger!" Ahh... those immortal words uttered by the Robot in the old TV series "Lost in Space" when danger was fast approaching. The robot could sense it before it got to them. And that's the key with danger: being able to recognize it and prepare for it before it ever appears. In this business, preparing for the worst all the time is the rule of thumb when it comes to danger. The only way you'll be able to deal with danger when and if it hits is if you are *prepared beforehand.* If you are prepared for something to occur, the element of surprise is taken away. The chance for an adverse action and its end result is much less if the element of surprise is diminished to a point where the action is rendered ineffective.

But danger is really not as prevalent in the PI world as the wandering imagination or the media might have you believe. In fact, it's a pretty safe occupation. When is the last time you heard of a PI dying in the line of duty? I rest my case. Is it because we are more prepared than, say, law enforcement, where officers put their life on the line each and every day? Not at all! You see, catching drug dealers, murderers, and other criminals is not the primary function of private investigators. It's not even a secondary function! Private investigators do not have the police power to arrest; nor should they. It's just not necessary and could even be detrimental. Our job is a definite delayed action reaction once we are hired. It's a business, and there's much less danger once the heat of the moment is over....and it's over ninety-nine-point-nine percent of the time by the time we are hired to investigate. Many of our investigations come months, or even years, after the main event has occurred.

But all of that is not to say that in the PI world there are no elements of danger, because there are; and I confidently confess that the degree of danger no doubt exceeds that of the common office worker. Criminal defense homicide investigators usually encounter the most danger, followed by those who investigate Racketeer Influenced and Corrupt Organizations (RICO) Act crimes for criminal defense attorneys. Undercover PI operatives can sometimes face danger. Drug investigation can be dangerous as well but they are few and far between as we are usually working for the *alleged* dealer's attorney. Domestic cases can become dangerous depending upon what kind of investigation is being conducted. Then there are the neighborhood canvasses, which can prove quite interesting at times. Surveillance, fraud, and background investigations can have hairy moments as well. But all things considered, you won't have much to worry about if you pay attention to detail and shoot straight (no pun intended).

About as dangerous as the average PI will have it is while conducting surveillance during a vehicle tail; you might get into a car accident if the brain is disengaged while driving, but that's about the extent of it if you know what you're doing. Worst part about crashing while following a subject would be the embarrassment you'd face when telling your boss and co-workers the story behind the crash (they'd probably cut you slack if you were injured, but even that's not guaranteed). Then you file all those claim forms, fight for a rental, argue with the insurance adjuster ...and settle for a lot less than what you intended just to end the agony. All because of a damned surveillance! Or you might get hassled and even arrested if the cops pull you over during a tail and you give them more grief than they're in the mood to handle. Other than that, unless you have the IQ of Ace Ventura, you're more likely to be okay if you are alert and aware.

The key to being prepared for potential danger is to imagine the situations you might encounter and role-play through them in your mind so you are ready if they occur. You need to have a great story to talk your way out of trouble and be able to leave (or run) with a smile on your face rather than ending up with a lump on the head. It's all about the art of communication and being street smart. If you can talk to the street bum one minute and then to a corporate president the next, while maintaining the dignity and respect of both, you won't have a problem. If you run across the street to avoid the bum or to run into the "pres," then... well, get a job in corporate America and become a sycophant kiss ass. It won't work in the PI world and you'll end up with your butt whipped on a regular and routine basis. Plus, your brother and sister PI's will silently abhor you, and some will publicly hammer you, including me (I've been known to hammer a few PI's that were deserving of a public thrashing and I make no apology for it).

And what about PI's and guns? This is the great myth in the PI sky: that PI work is dangerous and we all carry guns to ward off the danger. Hogwash! Many PI's don't even have gun permits, much less carry a gun. The fact is most PI's don't need to carry guns. The vast majority of cases PI's will investigate over their lifetime will not necessitate packing a firearm. In fact, it's detrimental. Carry a firearm and you should be ready to use it. Pull a gun and you should be prepared to pull the trigger. Although I might be prepared to pull the trigger if I have to, I'll never be prepared to deal with the consequences. And neither will you. And what happens if you are involved in a scuffle, the gun goes off, and someone gets shot? What happens when an innocent bystander gets killed? Your life as a PI will immediately cease – no questions asked, and you can take that to the bank. The first thing that'll happen if you shoot someone is you *will* be arrested. The questions will come *after* the arrest. The incident and the arrest will be big news, front-page stuff. Even if you shot in self defense, have witnesses to attest to it, and the DA files no charges, you'll end up getting sued by the injured party or by the estate of the deceased. And what about the clients; especially insurance companies, attorneys, and corporate types? Do you think they'll be banging down your door when they read the newspaper and see your picture plastered on the front page, especially if you're in handcuffs? Do you think your clients will want you working on their cases wondering if someone else will get shot? I don't think so. Your PI days will be over and your career will be devastated. Your agency's survival might be questionable as well. And what will happen to your co-workers if the agency goes under? Wow! Lots to think about.

Most of the PI's that carry guns do so because they have an ego that needs to be satisfied. Those that say they feel naked without it are fools. I rarely carry a gun and I investigate homicides. Since 1988, I have always had an active homicide investigation open, yet I can count on one hand the times I had a legitimate need to carry (usually at night in high crime, low income areas where there is high risk to life or limb). And I can't carry a badge! I have a business card, an ID card, and little ol' me. I do have a license to carry large-capacity firearms because there are times when it's necessary to have the protection of the weapon, but only to protect and defend oneself as a last resort. I let my common sense get me out of hot spots rather than using the big stick or a threat to use it. No question it's much safer, and the professional liability insurance premium ends up being much cheaper.

Talk about danger, being alert, and staying alive. I was a living example of it during one homicide investigation. Crazy stuff was happening to me when I was investigating the murders of Emile and Anna Duclos of Winchendon, MA in the case of Commonwealth v. John Smith[1]. I never said much about it because I didn't want to worry my family. As it turns out, they would have had nothing to worry about even if I had told them because I'm still alive and well (although I'm sure there are those out there that wish I weren't). So I figured it best not to tell anyone. I can't recall if I even told the attorney I was working for at the time, but I might have.

I was working on behalf of John Smith, a co-defendant charged with first-degree murder. The victim's son, Billy Duclos, was the other defendant. Billy, and Billy alone, planned and executed the brutal murder of his parents one night in May of 1989. They were in their bedroom, getting ready to go to sleep, when Billy shot them, execution style. It was a heinous crime, one of the worst I've seen. And he tried to pin the crime on John Smith and had, I'm sorry to say, some degree of success in doing so. In the end, though – after a trial conviction based entirely on Billy's testimony and Smith's police statement that he was on the property sleeping in a barn some seventy five yards away from the main house when the shootings occurred – an appeal (thank God) was successful in overturning his conviction. Although defense attorney Larry O'Connor lost at trial, his masterful *Motion to Suppress* [the statement of John Smith], the subsequent hearing, and the judge's mistaken ruling were the basis of the appeal.

Smith was going to be re-tried when Billy, once again, did something real stupid while in the slammer: He tried to have Smith "whacked" in jail. Duclos was convinced that he needed to kill Smith and make it look as if it were a suicide. Billy planned to have Smith killed and then somehow plant a forged suicide note next to the body. In this note, Smith would admit to the Duclos killings. Billy thought he would then have a "get out of jail free" card. Fortunately, this diabolical scheme didn't quite work out. Duclos got caught as a fellow inmate ratted him out, and coupled with his murder convictions, he'll never see the light of day.

In any event, I managed to talk Smith into pleading guilty to manslaughter prior to his second trial even though he was only guilty to being an accessory after the fact. I guess Smith trusted me more than his new trial attorney, or the district attorney, who were trying to get him to accept the plea. Larry Murphy was the Assistant District Attorney on the case. Murphy is a good man and an excellent trial attorney known for exhaustive preparation and honest, fair dealings with defense attorneys, investigators, police, and victims. I had a decent working relationship with Larry at the time and still do. Larry and defense attorney Gregg Schubert called me in on the day of trial to talk to Smith because he didn't know what to do; plead guilty to manslaughter or go to trial? I was loath to have him plead guilty to a crime he did not commit but I helped him realize the value of years outside of jail versus rotting away in jail for the rest of his natural life. So Smith reluctantly agreed to plead out after I begged him to do it. He was stuck on principle and the fact that he didn't kill Emile and Anna Duclos. Smith reiterated he knew nothing of the murder plan, not to mention he was not in the house until after the deed. And there was not one shred of physical evidence that put Smith in the second floor crime scene. But Smith had already served a lot of time awaiting trial and he'd be out of jail within eight or nine years if he pleaded to manslaughter rather than risk another first degree murder conviction. Smith was only guilty of being an accessory after the fact of murder, but could have been convicted of first degree murder a second time if the jury thought he was in with Billy on a joint venture. Although he didn't fully understand the legal theory of "joint venture," Smith did understand the meaning of "rolling the dice" with his life. I helped him to understand the meaning of freedom. He was smart and did the wise thing to assure he'd get out of jail while he was still young. John F. Smith was nineteen years old at the time the murders took place. He's now thirty four and free, living as normal a life as is possible outside of jail. I feel good about that, even though he ended up doing almost eleven years in jail rather than just the seven years he might have served had he been convicted of being an accessory after the fact. But the jury was hearing a murder charge and not an accessory charge! What would you do if faced with this dilemma? Roll the dice on life? Or plead to a crime you did not commit to regain your life? Smith made the right decision, but he still got screwed! John Smith did time for a crime he absolutely *did not* commit. And I feel bad about that!

Why am I telling you this? Because it was my job to show that Duclos wanted his parents dead. Smith had no motive, but Duclos did. In fact, he had a number of them. I investigated, uncovered, and obtained the details of each one over time. I found out that Billy had previously planned to kill his parents and make it look like an auto accident long before the shooting scheme. We had an expert inspect the parent's automobile and he found tampering with the brake lines. I investigated the insurance money motive of a burned barn that Billy wrongly thought was his – his parents took the money and didn't give him a dime. Although they let him rebuild the barn, Billy was incensed. Billy couldn't stand rules and his parents were strict disciplinarians, especially his mother. Duclos was repeatedly punished for minor and trivial matters and he couldn't take it anymore. Billy was at the breaking point. There were plenty of motives on his part, and Duclos *was* the sole planner. But he needed someone to take the fall so Smith became a "patsy." Billy did the only cowardly thing he could do when he got caught – blame Smith for the whole thing. Too bad Smith just didn't walk home from the barn when he heard the shots. He went into the house and Billy, holding a gun in his hand, asked Smith to help him out and help get rid of the guns. Smith was young and gullible and helped Duclos. Instead, he should've gone to the police and told them the truth. The good thing is that there was not one shred of physical evidence to link Smith with the actual crime. Why? Because Smith wasn't upstairs where the shootings occurred. The theory of defense was Smith didn't do it and only helped Billy after the fact because he felt threatened. It was a sad story but the case facts were strong. Then one day, the defense investigation turned dangerous. In fact, it was life threatening.

Throughout the lengthy investigation, I was receiving death threats by phone. Every so often, I'd get a phone call at the office from a man who would say "you'll end up just like Anna Duclos if you don't watch yourself" or "better watch your back" - threats like that. The crime scene pictures of Anna Duclos were not pretty. Half of Anna's head was blown off so I reasoned that someone might want to shoot me in the head, but I never did take it seriously. I did not report the calls...what could the cops do? The only one I told for sure was my wife. She reassured me, but I knew she was worried. Then one afternoon during the investigation, I decided to go to the Worcester Country Club driving range to hit golf balls and get a respite from the case. Little did I know (and I should have known), someone was watching me. The range at WCC is somewhat isolated from the pro shop and club house. I was alone and had been out there about fifteen minutes. There are railroad tracks that abut the driving range to the north. Off in the distance approximately two hundred fifty to three hundred yards northeast of me, I saw a person on the tracks. I couldn't tell if the person was a male or a female. I saw that person raise an object to shoulder level. The object looked like a rifle so I just started sprinting and zigzagging. At the same time I started to run, I heard pops and projectiles whizzing past my head. Terrified, I ran as fast as I could to the pro shop and told someone to call the police. By the time the cops got there, whoever had been up on the tracks shooting at me was long gone. I could never prove someone was even there, much less who it was, but I suspect the person was sent by Billy Duclos. And I have a good idea of who it might have been.

You had better believe that I carried my gun everywhere I went for the duration of that investigation. I got one last death threat after the incident at WCC. I told the guy that was calling that he had better not miss again because the next time I'd make sure he'd be the one with a bullet in his head. I'm grateful the next time never came. The reason I'm alive today is I was alert and aware of my surroundings. I was paying attention, and I thank God for that. The danger passed, and I really haven't carried my gun much since then. And I can't recollect a time when I needed any kind of weapon, even at WCC the day someone actually shot at me.

There's a saying out there "Don't worry about the threats you hear, worry about the ones you don't hear." I don't know who said it, but I'm here to tell you to also listen to the ones you hear! That's just common sense. But you don't need to carry a gun to ward off danger or threats. It's the wrong reason to carry and it only invites danger.

I guess I have to confess that I'm reasonably secure in what I do and who I am so I'm loath to carry any weapon except my brain, which I can't help but carry anyway. Remember, the strongest weapon is your mind. Use it well and danger will be averted and the wisdom to know when to stand and when to run will come easy. Be prepared!

2
SILENCE IS GOLDEN

If I were to try to...answer all the attacks made on me, this shop might as well be closed for any other business.

Abraham Lincoln

You know the saying: "Loose lips sink ships." I don't know who penned this quote but it is absolutely true. It is much better to listen than to talk. It is still better to listen and *then* to talk, and the less said the better. Listening is an art form that I have not yet perfected. I doubt I ever will, and there are not many others who have perfected it either. On the other hand, talking comes easy to a lot of folks, including me. Most people love to talk. No problem with that if it's intelligent talk, except the more time you take to talk the less time you have to listen. If you are going to talk, you had better know what you're talking about. If you have little or no knowledge about a subject, silence is golden. There are PI's that think they know everything about everything, which is impossible. The real problem is they actually believe it and then ego gets in the way of reason and that is dangerous. So, there are some rules about talking and listening in the PI profession you need to know about. And I intend to talk about them.

Rule one: *When dealing with a potential client or existing client on a new matter or possible assignment, listen to their problem first and then talk about how you might be able to help them if and only if you have knowledge about a potential solution.*

If not, silence is golden. It serves no useful purpose to pretend to have great knowledge and/or field competence in a particular area when you don't. You might be able to talk your way into the assignment, but, sooner or later, the incompetence will reveal itself and you will be embarrassed. For instance, if you are not a computer forensics investigator and a client has a problem in the area of computer forensics and needs an investigator, don't talk about how you can solve the problem unless you are a good computer forensics investigator, or until you can find someone to refer the client to – or, better yet, until you can hire someone to work for you (subcontracted specialist/expert) who is a good computer forensics investigator. I can't begin to tell you how many investigators take assignments and botch the investigation simply because they don't know what they're doing and get in over their heads. They could initially talk the talk, but could not walk the walk – and when found out, were told to take a walk.

I recall a client coming to see me after having spent thousands of dollars to have some other PI conduct a domestic surveillance on an ex-spouse who was hanging out with the wrong crowd and getting involved with drugs. The investigator kept losing the subject during vehicle tails, even with additional help. The job never got done right, and I found out why as soon as I learned the identity of the initial investigator. Although this man was qualified in court research and locating people, he had never conducted a complicated physical surveillance. He was afraid of getting burned. I say he was afraid of the case, which was a complex child custody matter. Whatever the reason (I suspect it was money motivated), he took a case he should have referred out. The client suffered. My agency re-worked the case and turned it into a success.

There's nothing worse than walking away from a client with your tail between your legs, empty handed and embarrassed. If you can help someone, tell him how and how much it will cost. If you can't help him yourself, tell him the truth. But also tell him you may be able to find a solution and to give you a few days to put a plan together. Then you call the expert investigator, make the plan, and get an estimate of cost. You then have another meeting with the person that needs your help and ask him to listen to your proposal. You might land the case. Making a little bit of money rather than a lot of money on one case is better than making nothing at all. Down the road, he may have a case you can handle without having to call in another investigator. Honesty and integrity is always the best policy.

Rule two: *When conducting an investigation, never reveal the name of the client unless authorized and only give out general information in order to potentially gain case evidence or gather more information.*

This deals with confidentiality. When you're dealing with things that are confidential, silence is golden. Unless you are specifically authorized, why would you need to reveal the name of the client? In some cases, especially criminal defense matters, you might want to tell a court clerk you are working for a particular attorney when seeking court records. You're more than likely going to get great service if you're working for a popular attorney. But what if you're not? It can be frustrating, for sure. If you believe it'll be helpful to drop an attorney's name, by all means do it but make sure you have authorization. Don't ever reveal the name of a client under any circumstances otherwise. People are paying you to keep their names out of it. When potential clients walk into my office or call me, one of the first things they ask about is confidentiality. You must assure it and maintain it at all cost. There are laws and ethical codes that bar the unauthorized release of client and case information. You could go to jail for doing it. Check your state PI licensing statute to see if there is a confidentiality clause as there is in Massachusetts (MGL Chapter 147 S. 28)[2]. And never, ever divulge any information to unauthorized individuals or entities without the permission of your client or unless an empowered authority directs or orders it. All individuals and entities are unauthorized to receive case information unless the client gives permission to release it or unless there is a court order. That's the rule I follow. It can be quite hairy at times.

I remember one situation when I received a deposition subpoena regarding a homeowner liability incident I investigated for an insurance company. A deposition is testimony under oath where an attorney from the opposing side asks questions about the case and the witness answers them; the attorney representing the side you're working for usually asks no questions if he/she is smart. The deposing lawyers, on the other hand, ask every question under the sun and want your life history and your first-born child too; it's an adversarial situation to say the least. So I called the client before the deposition and asked permission to release details of the investigation at the deposition. It's what I must do to comply with the law. Most clients tell you to answer the questions. There are times when the client tells you not to talk; this time was one of those times. The adjuster wouldn't allow me to release any information because he didn't believe the investigation I conducted was subject to disclosure. So I get to the attorneys office in Leominster, MA with my file. I talk to the lawyer hired by the insurance company to represent the insured and tell her I'm not allowed to release any information about the case. She's not surprised. She knew the law. Then a secretary led us into the law firm conference room that was no bigger than a jail cell. The attorney representing the plaintiff entered the room like a bullfighter would enter a bull ring, proclaiming his presence by the mere appearance of his muscle bound body. I had to do all I could to maintain my composure and not burst out laughing. I was sworn by the court reporter. The deposition began. We got through about two minutes of personal and work related identity questions and answers. I'll never forget the look of shock on the plaintiff attorney's face after he asked the first question about the case and I gave my answer. And to top that, the look on the defense attorney's face when she saw the reaction of the plaintiff attorney was priceless. He then said *"You're what?"* And I said "I can't answer the question." He asked why and I cited MGL Chapter 147, Section 28 and handed him his lunch on a plate: a copy of the law. He read the law:

> "Any person who is or has been an employee of a licensee and any licensee who divulges to anyone other than to his employer or as his employer shall direct, except before an authorized tribunal, any information acquired by him during such employment in respect to any of the work to

> which he has been assigned by such employer..... shall be punished by a fine of not more than five hundred dollars or by imprisonment for not more than one year, or both."

Astonished and obviously flustered, the bullfighter then looked at the other attorney and asked if I was going to answer any additional questions. She said she couldn't answer for me. Then the attorney asked me a similar question and I told him he'd have to ask the question before I could answer. He was clearly unprepared for this and became distraught. He began to sweat. I told the bullfighter lawyer that my client had not given me permission to release any information to him and that I doubted the deposition was "an authorized tribunal" as is the wording of the Massachusetts law. He argued for a moment and told the other attorney that he was going to court to get an order to compel me to talk. I looked at her and said, "I guess the deposition is over." The bullfighter stormed out of the room with a horn between his legs. He was clearly wounded. The other lawyer and I both got up and left. I never heard from this lawyer again. It appears to me that he never did get his order. It was a good laugh over beers that night.

I just love being questioned by lawyers in a deposition. They usually talk to me as if I'm some bastard stepchild. They find out real quick I'm a heavyweight contender. Lesson - never under estimate your opponent no matter who that person might be.

While it's against the law to release case file information about an investigation without permission, there are times when you must release information you have gathered in order to obtain other information to further the investigation; for instance, when you are trying to get truthful information out of a lying eyewitness and you confront the witness with what other witnesses have said to evoke a truthful response; or when you release personal and statistical data of a subject to get records from a public record custodian. It's a tough call sometimes but if you are to err, err on the side of confidentiality. So if you need to release information, make sure the client is informed and you have his or her consent. Otherwise, silence is golden.

Rule three: *Do not reveal confidential sources of information unless it is a real life or death situation.*

What good would any competent investigator be without confidential sources of information, paid and unpaid? We depend upon good work and information from these sources just as much as law enforcement relies upon paid and unpaid confidential informant information. We wouldn't be able to do our jobs nearly as well without informants, and law enforcement would be disadvantaged without them too; there is no difference between a PI informant and a police informant when you get right down to brass tacks. So don't give them up, unless, of course, you or another person is in a *real* life or death situation. Protect them like the cops protect their informants. Even if you are backed into a corner, don't reveal your sources. I'd go to jail before I'd release the names of my confidential sources. What good is my word as a PI and a human being if I sell them out? When I was a tenderfoot investigator, I'd often wonder what I would do if some judge ordered me to release the identity of my confidential sources. Do you know what you would do? Well I've made my decision. I'd have to respectfully decline unless it was a life and death situation. I suppose I'd also ask for consideration and request of the judge the opportunity to speak with his or her honor in chambers. What else could I do? I know I'd have my attorney with me if I knew it was coming. If I didn't, and the judge wouldn't give me consideration, I'd ask for time to consult with my attorney. And just what is a "real life or death situation?" Just what it says – life or death; that is if your life, or the life of another person, is in danger, and revealing the identity of the confidential source will make a life saving difference, then cough up the information. Otherwise, silence is golden. Thank God I've never been put in that position. I hope you never have to see it either.

Rule four: *When meeting with an attorney and their client, only speak when your input has been requested or is required.*

When a PI is lucky enough to have been invited to sit in on an attorney client meeting to discuss civil or criminal strategies, it should always be viewed as an opportunity to learn about the legal theories of the case, the case facts, and the opinions of the attorney and the client(s). The PI should never dominate or control the conversation. The main reason an attorney would want a PI in client meetings is to support the legal theories the attorney will outline, to plan investigative strategy, to listen to the clients concerns, and to provide investigation results and recommendations if investigation has been conducted. Attorney Peter Ettenberg, whom I will speak about in the coming chapters, is an attorney who routinely has me accompany him into conferences with criminal defense clients. I can't tell you how invaluable these meetings have been for all involved, especially me. To be honest, I consider myself lucky to be there. Peter outlines the case theories, tells of the contacts and substance of conversations he has had with the district attorney on the case, explains the law in a way the client understands it, and he listens to his clients and their loved ones about as well as I've observed anyone listen to anyone. Peter also requests my input, supports my recommendations regarding investigative theories and themes, and helps me to understand the legal issues, such as certain laws, rules of evidence, and legal procedure. I take a lot of notes, dig for discovery materials, and sometimes act as the voice of factual reality if the client ignores the evidence.

Here's an example of a difficult situation that had Peter and me pulling our hair out during one case[3]. And the truth of the matter is we don't have much hair to pull, even between the two of us.

I nickname some of my tougher, more interesting cases, and this one was called "Mommy Dearest." It wasn't tough because of the case facts. It was tough because of the client and her mother. The client was a defendant in a criminal complaint of three counts of larceny over $250.00 in a District Court in Worcester County. This thirty five year old female convenience store manager alleged she brought three deposits of store receipts to the bank on three consecutive nights and deposited the receipts into the bank night deposit repository box. Eventually, the store learned the deposits were never received by the bank and an investigation was launched by the police, the bank, and store security. Fifteen grand was missing. How could this happen? The convenience store manager was the mother of a teenage daughter with an excellent three-year work history at the convenience store; her husband was disabled and collecting disability. She admitted that she was the last person having possession of the night deposit bags, made out the deposit slips, counted the receipts, and recorded the deposits into the company computer. A key is required to open the night repository drop box. She stated she went to the bank on three consecutive nights, opened the night repository drop box with the key, placed the bags in the night deposit box on the outside of the bank, made sure the bags dropped into the vault, and closed the box making sure it was locked. The bank says they never inventoried the deposits because they were never received. Opening the night repository vault inside the bank called for dual control combination opening and dual controlled inventory. The dual control policy at the bank meant two employees would have had to conspire to commit the larceny; then they would've had to steal the deposits on three consecutive days inside the bank. No question this was an unlikely, but not impossible, theft. The police investigation pointed to the store manager. There was enough evidence to charge her, so she was charged in district court. That's when Peter and I entered the picture.

If it's not the manager of the store, it must be someone from inside the bank... right? Fairly straight defense of SODDI (some other dude did it) or a plea arrangement. It wasn't so simple. Mommy Dearest (the mother of the defendant) came in and took right over. She had the money and, by God, she was going to control the defense and the investigation. *If my little girl says she didn't do it, then she didn't do it* was what we were dealing with and what we heard time and time again in many different ways. It was like a broken record. The father bought into it as well. They were in complete denial. It really didn't matter what the evidence revealed. The defendant claimed innocence and that was good enough for Mommy: "My little girl doesn't lie Mr. Lajoie." Well, she lied and I could tell she was lying from day one throughout the ordeal.

For almost two years, I investigated every aspect of this incident, every bank employee, employees of the convenience store (they had nothing to do with it because all along the defendant stuck to what she had told police in a signed statement- that she took the deposits to the bank and placed them into the night repository), past employees of the bank and the convenience store, the night deposit vault, and the camera systems at the bank and at the convenience store. It would have been simple if there was an outside camera on the night repository box but there wasn't; there wasn't even a camera on the outside of that side of the bank. Yikes! When we first met with the defendant, she wouldn't look me straight in the eye when talking about the incident. Her non-verbal movements pointed towards guilt; not only in the first meeting but in meetings throughout the defense investigation. It was clear that she was afraid of her mother, afraid to tell her mother the truth, and afraid of the consequences. Mommy, a good person but relentless in her incredulous disregard for direct and circumstantial evidence, was overbearing in the meetings. The defendant barely had a moment to breathe let alone talk. And me, well.... they came to hate me. I was always the bearer of bad news. I was the bad guy in the meetings and Peter was the good guy. Mommy questioned everything, including our motives, and enhanced wild theories. Still, Peter and I were resolute and allegiant in doing our jobs. We would defend this girl right to the end. The problem was we would have had to ignore certain evidence, evidence that hammered the jail door shut. I also had a problem ignoring the fact that the defendant had taken a polygraph examination and failed miserably. Mommy forgot about that real quick. In the end, I was the one who cleared the mess up. During one of the many meetings (Peter wouldn't do a meeting on this case without me except at the end), Mommy Dearest said, "if you can't find evidence that she didn't do it, find me evidence that she did it." The case broke at the end of the investigation when employees (they weren't even employed by the store when the incidents occurred) of the convenience store were cleaning out a locked shed on the side of the store. They found the deposit bags inside the shed, hidden under some clothing and other items. There was over $3000 in cash inside one of the bags and some checks; $9,000 and change was missing. The police took the evidence, obtained statements, and did a short report. I was relieved to find that there was an outside camera at the convenience store that would show the shed every few seconds. The cops did no further investigation, but I needed to get more evidence for Mommy. I had to direct my focus on the client and Peter turned me loose to gather all the evidence. My job is to gather the facts regardless if it hurts or helps. In this case, the evidence that hurt us actually helped us. I had established a rapport with the regional security manager for the convenience store throughout the investigation. He was extremely cooperative. I wanted to look at the convenience store security tapes the day the regional manager told the store manager there was a problem with the deposits. Thank God he kept the tapes. Bingo! I found Mommy her evidence. Videotaped on the store security tapes during the heat of the initial police investigation was the defendant store manager driving onto store property and parking in front of the store, entering the store, going back out to her truck, retrieving a small shopping bag from inside her truck, and eventually walking to the shed. Then the camera showed her unlocking the shed, going inside the shed with the bag, and coming out a short time later empty handed. That same day, the convenience store relieved the store manager of her duties and took her keys...she couldn't get back inside the shed. It was obvious to me that she dumped the evidence because she was afraid of getting caught with it. The stuff, including the bag, remained in the shed for almost eighteen months. I had still photos printed from the tapes. I presented the evidence to Mommy. Mommy was still questioning the evidence, which was overwhelming. Peter was relieved. The store manager finally confessed to Peter that she did it. Peter told me she eventually confessed to Mommy; maybe so, but I couldn't see it happening. Peter then managed to get the case continued without a finding (CWOF) after the defendant agreed to pay restitution and have a period of supervised probation. No doubt she would have been sitting in jail for a long time had she been indicted and convicted at trial. The client made a big mistake one time in her life and could not face Mommy. Mommy paid all the defense costs (much more than what was taken). Guess who paid the restitution? Poetic justice I suppose. It was a high price to pay out of fear for ones mother, but no sweat off her back since Mommy was paying the bill. It just goes to show that good people can become blind out of love for their children. I'm glad I spoke up, even if I was hated and ridiculed all the way through. I saved Mommy's daughter from jail. I understand Mommy hugged Peter when all was said and done. I never even got a thank you. No problem....my thank you was a big fat check! I deposited it into the bank, really.......!

I try as best I can to only speak when my input is required or requested. Sometimes it's hard to stay silent if the client is critical as in the "Mommy Dearest" case, but professionalism and restraint must be maintained. This doesn't mean to roll over and play dead, but it does mean to control your impulses and try to be reasonable, even if the client is unreasonable. It serves no purpose to be hotheaded and emotional. In the meetings, be prepared to see the emotion pour out of the client and the client's family. During these periods, silence is certainly golden. And an understanding shoulder is also welcome comfort for some. Believe me, the attorney will appreciate your presence if you follow the rule and make him or her look good. I know Peter Ettenberg appreciates my being there to help out if needed, and I know the feeling on my side is most definitely mutual.

Rule five: *Do not directly or indirectly criticize, bad mouth, slander, or speak untruthfully about another private investigator so as to damage his or her reputation or adversely affect their business.*

To do so is unconscionable, unfair, and potentially libelous. Badmouthing another investigator is usually viewed as sour grapes almost one hundred percent of the time, especially if it is a dispute about business or clients. But some investigators just can't help themselves. Ego has a lot to do with it. I have to feel bad for these folks, but not as bad as I feel for the ones who are injured as a result of a violation of the rule. There are proper forums, authorities, tribunals, and agencies to which to formally complain if you have a complaint about a brother or sister investigator; use them if necessary. If not, silence is golden. Nuff said.

Rule six: *If you are being verbally attacked and the attacker is trying to elicit a negative response, be kind and considerate, and walk away in silence if possible.*

Kill 'em with kindness is the general tact with this kind of situation if you are unable to walk away from someone who is verbally abusive, insulting, critical, or accusatory. You may be sitting on a courtroom witness stand in a criminal case when the DA is hammering away at your credibility, personal reputation, and profession and you are unable to get away from it. If so, handle the situation with kindness and be considerate. If you're outside the same courtroom that same day and an investigator working the case for the state, or a family member from the opposing side, verbally insults you, simply walk away. Believe me; it's not worth the fight. Avoid a shouting contest at all cost. You're in business to serve the public and help others, and you'll be the goat if you let emotions get the best of you. There are people out there that will never understand, appreciate, or like what we do because they are close-minded and unprofessional. But it takes all kinds to make the world go `round. Sometimes I wish it didn't, but life is life. There are jerks everywhere you go. There's always someone willing to insult and trash your good name if it suits their purposes. Don't give in to it. I run into jerks all the time. There was a time I was in a police station looking at evidence and I was ridiculed by a police sergeant for something I had said about a police investigation during a case presentation I had made at an LPDAM (Licensed Private Detectives Association of Massachusetts) meeting in Worcester. I said nothing to this man and walked away. He was ill informed about what was said, but I wasn't going to argue with him on his terms in his territory. It would have been foolish to do so. Another time I was surrounded by members of a local gang known for violence and murder. They were inquiring why I was asking questions about a certain individual. I answered their questions with respect and didn't say too much more. I was able to walk out of the situation because I maintained professionalism and showed respect.

From time to time, you'll run into witnesses, subjects, nosy neighbors, police, and others that will not be kind to you. Walk away from them with a smile. In these situations, silence is golden. There are many more witnesses, subjects, nosy neighbors, and police who are professional, understanding, and will treat you with dignity and respect. Don't waste your time listening to the ones that get a kick out of harassing you. If you're bothered by it, you'll never get much done. Let it roll off your shoulders just like water rolls off an umbrella. Your burden will be that much lighter.

The rules of talking and listening in the PI world are simply my take on when to hear and when to be heard. Methinks it is sound advice and counsel. It's your choice to use them or trash them. No matter what profession you choose, there will be written and unwritten rules to follow with respect to proper conduct and protocol. Civility is always the best policy. So in my book, silence is golden. I guess the only time silence is not golden is if you make your living talking or when you're complimenting someone. So if you have something positive to say about someone, talk away. If not, walk away.

3

MESS UP, FESS UP

I never encourage deceit. And falsehood, especially if you have got a bad memory, is the worst enemy a fellow can have. The fact is, the truth is your truest friend, no matter what the circumstances are.

Abraham Lincoln

Unless there is some compelling legal matter at stake relating to a personal criminal complaint or indictment, when you mess up, you should fess up. And even then, when the truth is exposed....well, no comment. It takes a lot of courage and heart for most people to admit they're wrong, even when shown or proven to be guilty beyond all doubt. Why? I must confess I really don't know, but if I had to guess I'd say it has a lot to do with conviction (no pun intended), pride, ego, and/or the fear of getting caught and punished. Everyone wants to be loved, respected, trusted, and believed. Nobody wants to be ridiculed, scorned, criticized, disbelieved, and disciplined.

The ability to come forward and to admit faults, misconduct, impropriety, dereliction, malfeasance, and mistakes is a virtue. No question about it! To admit a mistake and be willing to face the fire is even more virtuous. There is no human being on the face of this earth, past and present, who hasn't made mistakes. But there are a lot less people who will admit to the mistakes, and even fewer who will admit to them and suffer the consequences.

Those who think they are perfect, believe they make no mistakes, and would never ever entertain the idea to admit a shortcoming or an error lack character and fortitude. And they usually spend an inordinate amount of wasted time trying to show the world how right they think they are or how wrong the other person or viewpoint is. People who fail to listen to constructive criticism and correct faults and mistakes are fools. I try to avoid them at all cost but it's virtually impossible because there are just too many of them. I know one thing; I don't want to be like them. I was young and naive once but have become older; and with age you hope to find some measure of wisdom. The sooner you figure this out, the better. God only knows I've made many mistakes in my life. I've paid the price for my mistakes and accepted the consequences. You should strive to make as few mistakes and errors as possible in your business and personal life. And when you do make a mistake, when you do mess up, I hope you'll have the courage and conviction to be honest with yourself and others and fess up. In some cases, it won't be easy. But you'll ultimately find that honesty and integrity will almost always win out over deceit and deception. And if it doesn't, whatever you lost or gained because of it wasn't worth keeping anyway.

Truth and trust is the number one factor in investigation. I call this the T² factor. If you cannot be trusted to seek and tell the truth in an investigation, then you definitely need not be an investigator. Lying to a supervisor, manager, or boss about some aspect of an investigation is to also lie to the client. In the PI profession, lying can mean possible death of the business and definite loss of the client. It also means reputation and credibility problems. I ask you this: Who would hire an investigator known to lie in a report? Would you? Of course not. And neither would any attorney, insurance company, business, or individual who has any sense.

Professional private investigators live by a Code of Ethics. The Code of Ethics outlines accepted practices and prohibits immoral, illegal, illicit, and unacceptable practices and behaviors. Almost every PI Code of Ethics I swear to live and die by says all reporting will be based upon fact and truth. It MUST be followed. If you don't follow it and lie about some aspect of an investigation and you are questioned about it, you must tell the truth and admit the mistake. To avoid the situation, *don't lie*!

Let me talk about just a few of the many investigative scenarios where it might be easy or tempting to mess up.

Surveillance: If you cut out of a surveillance operation at 2 PM, don't say 4 PM in the report. You're on your honor, and remember the T² factor. The agency is going to report and bill until 4 PM. Say you decide to report no activity from 2 to 4 PM and you cut out early because it's a perfect day to go play golf, go skiing, shop at the mall, or maybe have yourself a little afternoon delight or do whatever... you get the point. What happens when the subject gets in an automobile accident at 3:30 PM when you reported no activity and stated the subject remained in his house or at work? I think there might be a bit of a problem here! In addition to the lie, you are stealing from the agency and also from the client when the bill goes out. You just lied in two places, the report and the bill; definitely not a good practice. Don't do it! And if you mess up, fess up and suffer the consequences.

Reporting: Do not try to word a report to avoid telling the complete truth. Don't keep all the facts about a case to yourself because you know it hurts the client or the client's client, such as in the case of a criminal defense matter. Do not show bias toward one side of a case and prejudice to the other. Keep an open mind. Investigate and then report with neutrality in mind. You're not investigating to flavor a matter or situation one way or the other. Let an attorney, advocate or adjuster do what they want with the facts once you gather and report them. You're doing no one any favors by hiding facts that can have an impact. Tell it like it is. Load the canon with facts, but let someone else do the shootin'. If you leave something out of a report deliberately, or even unintentionally, you messed up. And if you mess up, fess up.

Identification: Identifying yourself as being a private investigator as opposed to a police investigator is paramount, especially when you are questioning anyone or seeking information from someone during an investigation. Never ever identify yourself as law enforcement. To say "I'm a detective" doesn't cut it because people can get the wrong impression, especially if you're also carrying a badge (illegal in some states). Pulling an ID card out with a badge and identifying yourself as simply "a detective" is messing up. Don't do it! Tell people who you are and give them a business card so there can be no question as to identification. Don't leave anything to interpretation. There is nothing in the law that I know of that requires you to tell people who you work for, but if they ask be up front and tell them. If you are secretive and clandestine about who you are (unless you are undercover or conducting a legal pretext), there will always be a question about your honesty and integrity.

When a potential witness asks who I work for, I always say this:

> "Regardless of who I work for, it doesn't change the facts of the incident and that's what I'm here to get – the truth. I'm not interested in favoring or even flavoring one side or the other. That being said, I'm a professional private investigator, hired by (fill in the blank) to obtain the facts, the true facts. If it hurts or helps the person that hired me or his client then that's just the way it is. I need your help because I can sense that you can add a level of understanding to what happened..."

You know what, it usually works. Remember – you catch more flies with honey. If you refuse to fully identify yourself when necessary and proper, you messed up. And when you mess up, you must fess up.

Here's a real life experience about identification and the various interpretations of identification:

I was working a homicide case in central Massachusetts in the 1990's known as Commonwealth v. Deborah Reid[4]. Deborah Reid had the best self-defense case I have ever encountered, yet she was still convicted of manslaughter (it makes one wonder if self-defense is actually a justifiable homicide as the law says it is). Reid was attacked by her lover in their Fitchburg, MA apartment with a heavy wine bottle. She retreated into a corner of the kitchen near the stove. Her lover was at least fifty pounds heavier and much taller than Deborah, and she was intoxicated. The aggressor pursued Deborah into the corner and raised the wine bottle over her head. As she was about to strike with the wine bottle, Deborah grabbed a kitchen knife from the stovetop and stabbed her lover one time on the left side of the torso. Her lover died. Deborah was arrested, prosecuted, convicted, and sentenced to prison at Framingham Correctional Institute in Framingham, Massachusetts.

Deborah Reid later became known as one of the infamous "Framingham Eight," a group of eight females incarcerated at Framingham Correctional Institute who had been abused and beaten by the ones they killed, but nevertheless were ultimately convicted (wrongfully in my opinion) of murder or manslaughter. They brought their cases to the Massachusetts Board of Pardons to have their sentences commuted based upon the defense of "Battered Woman Syndrome" and several were successful. Deborah Reid was not one of the successful ones, although they did reduce her sentence *after* she had been freed for serving her time. Talk about a meaningless victory.

In any event, I was interviewing key witnesses one day in central Massachusetts on the Reid case. I happened to make a cold call (unannounced visit) to an eyewitness – a young, adult male who was at the scene at the time of the incident. I identified myself as a private investigator and gave this guy my card. He never asked me for whom I was working, so I never told him. I did an interview and might have taken a statement. The information obtained was favorable for the defense. When the cops found out this witness had talked to me, they went to see him. The witness told the police that he thought I was a cop and that's why he talked. The cops told the district attorney working the case that I identified myself to the witness as law enforcement. The DA then sought to have me taken off the case and there was an actual hearing on it. Can you imagine? Nothing but pure smoke and malarkey. The whole thing was a complete waste of time because the witness was lying. His motive to lie was he didn't want to incur the wrath of the police so he found a convenient solution to use as an excuse to sanction giving up information to the defense. It wasn't too convenient for me! Joe LoStracco was the Assistant District Attorney prosecuting the case. He's still around and we now laugh about the hearing, but I wasn't laughing when it happened. It wasn't a joke. I understand that Joe was just doing his job. I took it well because I figured if they are that interested in taking me off the case, I must be doing my job. I wasn't *too* worried about it though and neither was my client.

In any criminal matter, police detectives have no business intimidating a witness; that's what I think happened in this case, although I could never prove it... just a gut feeling. The cops would never admit it. But that's okay because the witness and I know what really happened. The judge denied the motion of the DA after the hearing. I guess the judge didn't believe them. I stayed on the case and also helped out during the "Framingham Eight" appeal process. Deborah Reid is now a free lady. God bless her. She's another one that got screwed.

The lesson learned here is to tell people who you work for even though there is no law or obligation that says you must. It's a tough call sometimes because you want to get the information from a witness who you think might not talk if you tell him for whom you are working; but you certainly leave yourself open to criticism if you don't ID yourself properly. So just do it. Sometimes I write the name of the attorney I'm working for on the back of my card and leave it at that. But now I tell everyone exactly on whose behalf I seek information. It's really the best policy. In fact, it's the only policy. Don't get me wrong, I'd love to have as much information as is possible to obtain from *all* the witnesses in all cases, but if he or she chooses not to talk to me they'll have to answer to a defense attorney in court. It could go something like this:

Question: **"Did Mr. Lajoie come to your house?"**

Answer: **"Yes."**

Question: **"Did Mr. Lajoie identify himself as an investigator for the defense?"**

Answer: **"Yes."**

Question: **"And isn't it true that Mr. Lajoie asked you to tell him the truth?"**

Answer: **"Yes."**

Question: **"And isn't it also true Mr. Witness, you told Mr. Lajoie you didn't want to tell him the truth?"**

Answer: **"Well, not exactly."**

Question: **"Well, what exactly did you tell him?"**

Answer: **"I told him to get the hell out of here because I'm not talking."**

Question: **"And just what is it that you thought you had to hide from Mr. Lajoie?"**

Answer: **"I got nothing to hide."**

Question: **"Well then, please explain to the court why it is you thought it best not to tell Mr. Lajoie the truth?**

Answer: **"Because the cops told me not too!"**

You get the point. The defense attorney can have a field day with this witness. There's always a higher authority in which someone will have to explain his or her actions. Let it go at that and the chips will fall where they fall. Don't let it bother you otherwise.

Here's a hard life experience where I learned from my mistakes:

One day in my early PI years, I was seeking a mug shot of a potential rapist from a city police department close to Brockton, MA. I needed it because the rape case defendant on whose behalf I was working was wrongfully identified. I was working for an attorney named George Leary, who is now a well-respected juvenile court justice in Worcester, MA. So I traveled to this police department to see if they would provide a photo of a convicted rapist who may become the defense suspect of the case I was working. I knew that mug shots are Criminal Offender Record Information (CORI) and are not normally subject to release under the Massachusetts Freedom of Information Act (FOIA). The record custodian, however, has the option to release FOIA excluded records at his or her discretion in Massachusetts. So I sought to obtain the pictures. When I got to the police station, they were about to do a shift change. I gave the dispatcher my business card and told him who I was, where I was from, and what I was seeking. I waited a long time, perhaps thirty minutes. I assumed the dispatcher gave my card to the detective that finally came to greet me. That was my first mistake. My second mistake was made after the police detective took me into the back room where records were kept. He asked me what I needed and I told him this: "I'm a detective from Worcester working a rape case and I need some mug shots of a convicted rapist that you might have." He never asked me my name and I never offered it because I thought he had my card. I gave the detective the information about the rapist. He obtained the mug shots and an arrest record and gave them to me on the spot. I thanked him and was on my way.

About a month later, I found out there was a warrant issued for my arrest on charges alleging that I had impersonated a police officer. I immediately sought representation and had the warrant removed. But I still had to deal with a criminal complaint. The police alleged I lied to the detective and obtained the CORI information under false pretenses. That was their interpretation; I had a different one. The only way they could have gotten my name and address was from the *identifying business card* (my card) I had given to the dispatcher.

In the end, the complaint was dismissed, but it cost me $2,500.00 and my client had to return the pictures and arrest record to the police. It was a major hassle. And I had to eat crow with the client as well, which is never a good thing. But when you mess up, you fess up. I really wasn't too worried about my reputation with police at that time because I was young and stupid. But the mistakes I made in the handling of this matter are obvious. I should have given the detective a business card as well. I should have told him I was working a criminal *DEFENSE* case and that I was a *PRIVATE* detective. And if I had an ID card (MA did not issue ID cards to PI's at that time but they do now) I should have produced it. I also compromised the investigation and exposed my client's good name to risk. Thank God he understood.

Live and learn. I admitted the mistakes made but *did not* impersonate a police officer; I have never impersonated anyone and never will. Make sure you aren't tempted to do it because you could lose it all. Be proud of who and what you are and don't hesitate to tell police exactly who you are and what it is you seek. These people are not out to get you; they have a lot more to worry about than bagging an honest PI. And to tell you the truth, you're not even on their radar screen unless you break the law; even when you're working a big criminal defense case. More times than not, the police will help you out if they can so let's try hard to get by law enforcement deliberately trying to do you in. There's always some isolated incident on a case you might have worked where some officer has nothing better to do than to give you grief. But it just doesn't happen that often. In fact, it rarely happens, but when it does that's what you tend to recall. I want to recall the times when law enforcement personnel have helped me out in situations where I needed their help and cooperation. It is a much more frequent occurrence than you might think, especially when you treat them with dignity and respect. And if it's not happening for you, perhaps you might need to adjust your approach and attitude.

Eating crow, admitting to mistakes, and being truthful are tantamount in business and in life. It is especially true in the investigation business. Don't let your ego get the best of you. Don't let pride stand in the way of doing what is right. And please do not lie; lying hurts the profession, casting a murky shadow on all PI's. If you make an error or mistake during an investigation, tell your boss or client and stand tall for the consequence. It might not be as bad as you think. Nobody is perfect. No one person is beyond accountability. No one is bullet proof. If you mess up, fess up.

4
MENTORS

I should be the most presumptuous blockhead on this footstool if I for one day thought that I could discharge the duties which have come upon me...without the aid and enlightenment of one who is stronger and wiser.

Abraham Lincoln

I would be nothing without mentors. Who would be something without them? Most successful people would probably agree that their success was, in part, due to the advice, teachings, and wisdom of someone who took a special interest in them and unselfishly imparted their knowledge to them. There is usually more than one mentor over the course of ones lifetime, perhaps many. I have learned from my mentors, admired them, loved them, at times hated them, and have always respected them. I have had many mentors and teachers in my lifetime, as you've probably had as well. They have taught me, scolded me, counseled me, loved me, hated me, complimented and ridiculed me. They have trusted me and busted me. And there can be no doubt they have helped me become the person and investigator I am today. I owe to them my loyalty, friendship, admiration, and respect. I love them agape. And I consider myself lucky to have had these mentors and count my blessings many times over. They become your friends and then you eventually consider them like a brother or sister, mother or father. They pass onto you their compassion and wisdom. They help you become who and what you are. They lead you to a better tomorrow and help you through today. They mold your life and fine-tune your humanity.

First and foremost are my father and mother, Raymond and Coralie Lajoie, who gave to me the gift of life. And I owe them my life. My father has been a golf professional for more than fifty years. Up until his retirement in 1997, he was the head golf professional at Worcester Country Club (WCC), a private country club with a rich and diverse New England yankee tradition. He worked at least seventy hours a week for forty four years (talk about longevity and work ethic!) from March through December at the WCC because he knew he had to. He had no college experience and no formal occupational training. What he also knew as well as anyone else was the business of golf. When I was a pre-teen into my teen years, I despised his work hours. When everyone else was off (weekends, holidays, summers) he had to be on. As a kid I never saw him on the weekends or in the summer except Mondays, his usual day off. It was during my teen years that my Dad had me working for him at WCC, where I learned what I could of the golf business and determined rather quickly it wasn't for me. But it was here where I began to realize that nothing comes easy; there are no free rides; and you must work hard to get ahead. I also learned that thanks for a job well done doesn't necessarily come when you think it should. It was here where I met influential people who would help shape my life and help me in business, as you will soon read. I also learned how to play the game of golf well. I made a name for myself playing golf in amateur tournaments, particularly in central Massachusetts, and then while in the US Air Force in Europe. The golf lessons from my father that shaped my golf swing also shaped my life and are still an invaluable resource in business, in the real world, and in life in general. If it wasn't for my Dad, I wouldn't have found the talent I had for the game. I wouldn't have met the influential business people who were and are the members of the WCC, some of whom are my clients today. And I wouldn't have met Larry O'Connor, my first criminal defense investigation client and mentor. I also would have had less time with my Dad. And I certainly wouldn't have believed the many life lessons my father was talking about through his experiences at WCC if I hadn't seen them with my own eyes; things like loyalty, commitment, respect, restraint (it comes hard for the both of us), charity, work ethic and the difference between right and wrong, good and bad. My mother was behind him one hundred percent and had no choice but to stay at home to care for four children, one (Lori) who was mentally challenged. She was and still is a statue of perseverance. Eventually, she went to work at WCC and joined Dad running the business and servicing the WCC members. She's as much a part of me as he and I've learned an awful lot from them both. The lesson here is to take advantage of opportunities and experiences at a young age because, more times than not, it'll help you later on in life and in business.

In the private investigation profession, loyalty within the average PI agency is almost non-existent. It took me almost ten years to assemble a staff that is completely loyal to the agency and me. I am grateful to all my employees. I respect their commitment and dedication. I care deeply for them all and am extremely appreciative for their loyalty and faith. But above all, there is one employee that is loyal beyond imagination – my devoted wife, Susan Lajoie. I learn from her every day. She's another voice of reason that catches my ear and is a fabulous mentor. It's great to have someone to bounce ideas off, no matter how crazy or foolish, or at whatever time of the day or night. She has a soft touch and can clearly help me with the compassionate side of an issue. If I'm wrong, she'll tell me. If I'm off line, she'll reel me in. If I persist with an irrational thought process or action, she'll stop it. If I'm right, she'll defend me to the end. And she sometimes acts as a buffer between the employees and me. She was with me when we discussed my leaving a secure job to start a business from scratch in 1988. She was with me when I had some personal and business problems in 1992 and 1993. She was with me when I had medical issues in 1997. In 1999, she came to work for Lajoie Investigations, Inc. full time. It was, without a doubt, the best thing that ever happened to the company; the other employees will certainly back me up on it. You see, she's not a spousal control freak. She doesn't want to be the big boss. She's content with managing the administration of the agency without making waves. And she's a terrific accounts receivable collection agent. I rarely have an invoice over sixty days. Ninety percent of our invoices are paid within three weeks. Best thing of all is we really stay out of each other's way while working. Some days, she buries herself at the opposite side of the building and we hardly see each other. Only God knows why she loves me, but I know why I love her. And I don't love her because I need her. I need her because I love her. She's my strength when I'm weak, my courage when I'm scared, my voice when I'm mute, my spirit when my soul seems empty, and the mother of our three lovely children. She's simply the best. Everyone needs somebody like her, my father, and my mother. Without them I am nothing.

I worked for the United States Air Force (USAF) for six years after high school. I had many mentors over those six years. I can't even begin to tell you how grateful I am to all my USAF mentors. In 1980, I was stationed at RAF Mildenhall in England (about seventy miles north of London). There was a full bird US Army Colonel stationed at Mildenhall named Colonel Ivey- first names were seldom used when I was in the military and I don't recall his, although I wish I did. He taught English Composition 101 for the University of Maryland extension college at the neighboring RAF Lakenheath base. I enrolled in his college night class just to get it out of the way. It was my first college class. Ivey was a complete ball-buster. There is no one on the face of this Earth that I have met since who knows English grammar and composition better than this man; no one even close. I was writing "D" grade composition papers when I first entered his class. I hated this guy. I'd turn in what I thought was a great paper and, by the time he finished with it, the paper would be "red marked" so that you couldn't see the margins any more, on both sides of the page! He'd circle the grammatical problem, write the grammar or the punctuation rule in the margin, along with the textbook chapter to read to figure out and correct the mistake. All mistakes had to be corrected or he'd fail the paper. Nor was there an upgrade in the original grade. Half the class dropped out after a few weeks but I toughed it out. He even made us talk about the papers and grammar corrections in front of the class. At the end of the semester, I was writing "A" grade papers. Colonel Ivey announced to the class at the end of the course that I was the only student he had in over ten years of teaching that came in writing "D" and left writing "A" grade papers. It felt good, but I could have cared less about the grade. What mattered most is the fact that this man had taught me how to write well in just twelve weeks time. When I left the USAF, I breezed through college with A's because I could write a complete sentence and speak to an audience. The composition lessons taught in Colonel Ivey's class have served me well to this day in my investigative report writing and speaking presentations. And now the employees at Lajoie Investigations know where I got the idea to "red mark" the reports they ask me to review. So, if you find yourself having trouble putting your words and thoughts into a cohesive written report or paper, do yourself a favor and go out and find a Colonel Ivey at the local college and enroll in the class. It'll be tough for a short stretch, no doubt, but the benefit will last a lifetime.

Karyn Macgillivray, Esq. stands just four feet ten inches tall and probably weighs all of ninety five pounds but there's no question she's a heavyweight in the art of negotiation and insurance litigation issues. Karyn was – and still is – the Litigation Manager of the OTA (Other Than Auto) and Litigation Department at Commerce Insurance Company (CIC) of Webster, MA when I landed in her department in early 1988. I had just done a stint as a road investigator/adjuster for CIC and took a position in her unit to learn all lines insurance and litigation claims handling. Her department was small but well respected. Only the best claims investigators and adjusters are selected to fill positions in this department. In 1988, there were five of us, and Karyn. Now, there must be close to thirty, and Karyn. And she hasn't changed a bit except she is much wiser. Anyway, she was a first class mentor and she still offers advice when I ask. As a manager at CIC, it was she who taught me how to read and interpret complicated all lines insurance coverage and liability policies and apply loss facts to coverage. It was she who would have no hesitation to knock me down a few notches when I was getting a little too big for my britches. I remember one time in a meeting she told me to "shut up" in front of the four other members of the unit because I was dominating a conversation – a little embarrassing – but boy did it work. It was she who taught me the art of negotiation and dispute resolution. And it was she who gave me the opportunity to fulfill the American dream of starting my own company. While working at CIC, especially in Karyn's department, I had the opportunity to review many investigative reports, assign outside investigations to PI agencies, and consult with many investigators and experts. I saw a void in central Massachusetts and believed I could provide a much better product to insurance companies and attorneys than what I was seeing out of the agencies providing investigation to CIC. I did my research, saved my money, and eventually decided to take the risk and leave that secure job at CIC to start Lajoie Investigations, Inc in 1989. The experiences at CIC, the number one property-casualty insurer in Massachusetts at present, were invaluable. Karyn's willingness to write me that letter of recommendation to obtain my state PI license was vital to the success of my starting an agency. I had to ask her to help me, but it was not difficult because Karyn is approachable and had always been open with me up to that point. I had no reason to believe she would not be supportive, but I admit I was a bit nervous. So one day I told her about my future plans and dreams. She then asked me, "What if it doesn't work out?" I told her I'd come back to CIC if she'd have me but I had to give it a go. She then said, "You know we won't be able to use you." I clearly understood that no insurance company was going to let a valued employee leave only to become an authorized vendor. What message would that send to other employees? I told Karyn that I didn't expect anything from CIC other than good will. I also told her my goal was to make my future agency the best in the business realizing CIC might take notice and consider using Lajoie Investigations. You know what, Karyn Macgillivray did write that letter of recommendation. She was also interviewed by the Massachusetts State Police Licensing Unit as part of my licensing background investigation. When I finally obtained my PI license, I went to Karyn and thanked her and gave notice. She asked me to stay an additional month and I agreed. I worked hard for Karyn and CIC right up until the day I left. Two years later, CIC became a client and they've been with me ever since. I'll always owe a debt of gratitude to Karyn Macgillivray and the Commerce Insurance Company. When I started my work at CIC, they had fewer than two hundred employees. Now they have more than two thousand because they have bright, energetic employees and a top notch, business minded upper management team. They gave me the chance to succeed and the knowledge to investigate. I am grateful and appreciative to them for the experiences and the opportunities. You too can have a similar relationship with your employers but there has to be mutual trust. Don't burn any bridges because you reap what you sew. And remember, as Karyn would always say, "you catch more flies with honey than you do with vinegar."[5]

Lawrence S. O'Connor, attorney extraordinaire, was my father figure in the criminal defense investigation arena. Larry is retired now and I seldom see him, but there's not a day that passes when I don't think about him. He was a street beat cop in Worcester, Massachusetts who worked his way up to the homicide unit where he became a first class homicide detective. He eventually left when he earned a law degree to become an assistant district attorney prosecuting criminals. After many years in the DA's office, Larry left for private practice where he eventually established his own firm and became a master at representing defendants charged with homicide. Of course, he worked other cases as well, both criminal and civil. Larry was also a member of the Worcester Country Club (thanks Dad) and I was an acquaintance of his since my high school days. Well-respected, dignified, intelligent, witty, and street smart, boy could Larry talk to a jury. He could also write pre-trial suppression motions with the best of 'em. Larry knew I was an investigator/adjuster at CIC. One day in October of 1988, I'm sitting at my desk at CIC and I get a phone call from Larry. Larry said he subpoenaed one of my large loss auto accident files (his client was a CIC insured who was charged with leaving the scene of a personal injury accident) where I had conducted a rather detailed field investigation. Larry reviewed my work and was rather impressed. He commented, "You do a better job than the cops." Larry then asked me to consider doing some investigation for him on a criminal defense case on the side. I told him I'd love to help him out but I had to pass it by Karyn Macgillivray. Loyalty to CIC was first and foremost but, if there was no conflict, I couldn't see a reason why I wouldn't be able to help him out. Lucky for me that Karyn didn't either. Best thing of all is that I'd be getting paid – $40 an hour plus expenses. My dream was beginning to take root. I was apprehensive but confident I could work independent. So I called Larry back and told him I'd do it, but I had no PI license. Larry told me not to sweat it and to leave the technicalities to him. I set up an appointment to see him on November 1, 1988. I had never before worked a criminal defense case – I didn't have a clue. What I did have was a solid foundation of investigating complicated insurance civil cases where criminal charges overlapped by having been filed against a claimant or insured. I walked into Larry's office thinking he'd need help in a simple assault and battery or a DUI (driving under the influence of alcohol). Larry was in the conference room with Jimmy Rosseel, his partner. The conference table was completely covered with police reports and other discovery. I asked Larry about all the paperwork and he told me it was the recent Gardner, Massachusetts murder case. I said I had read all about it in the papers. It was front-page news because the victim was a former high school principal and the suspects had fled and were apprehended in Las Vegas. He then said "Congratulations, you are now the chief homicide defense investigator for Gail Blair,"[6] one of the defendants in the case. I was floored! It couldn't be happening to me. A highly respected homicide defense attorney in central Massachusetts wanted me as his murder investigator. Oh boy...the sweat set in. I got nervous. I was admittedly apprehensive. Larry saw I was dizzy and told me to sit down and relax. He reassured me that I had what it takes to investigate any matter, including homicides. He promised to provide the mentoring in areas where I needed help. Larry O'Connor fulfilled his promise to me ten times over in the next ten years. Within days, Larry had a court-approved motion naming me as his investigator and approving payment not to exceed $2,500. He told me he'd get more money approved when (not if) the initial monies where exhausted for investigative service hours and expenses. Larry had reviewed the private detective licensing laws and showed me where there was an exemption to having a private detective license if I was court appointed. Reality began to set in. I was now partly responsible for the life of a female who was charged with first-degree murder. My first criminal defense case was a homicide investigation. It was scary, but Larry was with me every step of the way. He taught me how to index and organize a homicide defense file for investigation (and I also use the same indexing system for large civil cases and other criminal defense matters). Larry went over theories of defense and investigation themes. He taught me about weapons, forensics, evidence, statements, street rules, investigative and criminal procedures, reputation, credibility, autopsies, and just about everything you need to know about investigating a criminal case, especially homicides.

Few knew more than Larry O'Connor, because he had seen and done it all. And he unselfishly passed just a little of his wisdom and knowledge to me. I am humbled and grateful. He must have seen something in me because now I'm lucky enough to say that others consider me one of the best in the business of criminal defense homicide investigation. Larry is a master and I was, without question, privileged and honored to have been his servant. He now follows my career and he tells me he reads about me in the papers. Larry is the reason I am what I am. Part of him is in me and I am proud to call Larry O'Connor my supreme investigative mentor.

I would certainly be remiss if I did not mention Peter Ettenberg, Esq., Senior Partner at the Law Offices of Gould and Ettenberg; W. Theodore "Ted" Harris, former attorney at law and king of the closing argument; Brian Schofield, Commerce Insurance Company Special Investigations Unit (SIU) Manager; and Stephen Gordon, Esq. of Gordon & Gordon. They are contemporary mentors with whom I share my ideas, thoughts, and concerns. They, in turn, offer friendly advice and point out when I'm off the mark. I've known all four for a long time and have worked with each one of them on sensitive business and personal issues. I work closely with Peter, Brian, and Steve just about every day. Ted is in Las Vegas now and I don't see him much, but we stay in touch. They are wise men, good human beings, and their advice is extremely valuable. All four can be trusted. I consider them good friends. I am grateful to each for their friendship, support, and much more.

I also would like to mention Julius "Buddy" Bombet, Warren J. Sonne; Katherine "Kitty" Hailey, Diane Cowan, and, of course, Herbert Simon, all contemporary colleagues, most of them private investigation agency owners and authors. They help me when I'm lost, advise me when I ask, and have unselfishly shared their wisdom. I consider them close friends. They willingly share knowledge that enables me to see differing viewpoints so I can make sound business decisions. We trust each other. And trust is a very rare commodity indeed, especially among competing investigators.

I know I mentioned one teacher, but must give credit to all of them. Without teachers where would we be? Where would I be? Where would you be? To the Ruth Bositis's, Neil Brophy's and Tony Volpe's[7] of the world, we owe to you our greatest gratitude and appreciation.

You cannot succeed without mentors. There's not much more I can say. Open your heart and mind to their compassion and knowledge and you should find much success in business and in life. I know I have. And don't forget to thank them.

5
BUSINESS IS BUSINESS

Every man has his own peculiar and particular way of getting at and doing things, and he is often criticized because that way is not the one adopted by others. The great idea is to accomplish what you set out to do.

Abraham Lincoln

Business is business; family is family; friendship is friendship; pleasure is pleasure. Be sure to keep it that way. If you're not careful, mixing this stuff is like mixing a Molotov cocktail: it could blow up in your face. When you are set and ready to start your business (no matter what kind of business) you must stick to the business at hand, pay attention to the details, and make sound business decisions that will affect the operation and life of your company in a positive way. If you are not completely ready to live, eat, drink, sleep (what sleep???!!!), digest, and _ _ _ _ the business, then it is more than likely to fail, so don't bother wasting your time, effort, and money. You'll become aggravated and depressed. Yes, there is always some person out there that is ready to make the sacrifice and take the risk necessary to start up and operate a private investigation company. It's done everyday on every corner of the Earth. But not all of them make it. In fact, most of them just barely survive, if at all. So if you, or your significant other, are unable to make considerable sacrifice and take substantial risk, then don't do it. Do yourself a favor, go work for someone else so the business headaches will be theirs and not yours. And if you are meeting resistance from your significant other, either get rid of the idea of starting a business or get rid of the significant other. You can't have it both ways unless there is unyielding support. It's a harsh reality but it's business. And business is business.

There are few people who have started a business and succeeded without some support or help. Then there are the ones who are warned by naysayers, significant others, friends and family: "Don't do it!" But they do it anyway, and almost all of them fail miserably. The small percent that succeed with no support are usually driven by greed and money. What makes them happy is money and money alone. I'll tell you one thing I know for sure – I don't want to be like them. And if you're listening to me and understand what I'm getting at, neither do you. Sure I like money. Who doesn't? In fact, I love money. I love having it and I love spending it. You need money to survive. You need to pay the bills. You need to buy food, and so on and so forth. But the relentless quest for money seldom makes long-term business success a reality. In fact, it's usually just the opposite. Oftentimes, the ones motivated by greed and money step all over others in their inexorable pursuit to climb the ladder, forgetting that at some point they may be forced to come down. It's not a pretty picture and the descent isn't too pleasant either.

The formula for business success is exhaustive planning, good human relationships, solid support from friends, family, and the people that help you along the way, a stable client base, competent vendors and service providers, loyalty and support from employees, and hard work. Hard work is the key element followed by a stable client base. And there is one other important element that is absolutely necessary: belief in self. If you don't have confidence (be careful not to confuse this with ego) and believe in yourself, then it is likely any business you start will fail. Starting and succeeding in business is much more than just saying it and even believing it; it's living it, doing it, and setting an example of it. Ben Franklin once commented, "Well done is better than well said"[8]. And that goes right to the heart of it. Doing it and doing it well. Talk is certainly cheap, but doing it is golden. If you know how to do something well, it will inspire confidence and ignite the belief in your ability to accomplish what you set out to do – that is to start an investigation services business. And how do you start an investigative agency from scratch? Well, I can only speak for myself, so I'll make five suggestions and share a bit of knowledge based upon my experiences.

First, you must learn how to investigate. And I mean investigate. You must be a good, solid investigator. Coming out of high school I enlisted in the military (I recognized what I needed at the time was discipline). Then I worked for a security agency while attending college (I knew I desperately needed a college education). After I graduated with a BA degree in history, political science, and philosophy, I went to work as an adjuster/investigator for an insurance company (I needed to make money and gain experience). I had no idea I wanted to be an investigator until I worked in the insurance claims industry conducting investigations and adjusting property-casualty claims. Others who have an interest in investigation work are law enforcement officers, court appointed investigators, public or federal defender investigators, corporate in house investigators, military investigators, law firm investigators, and investigators for established investigative agencies. People who work for these entities usually receive training and are taught the art and science of investigation. If you can't investigate well, don't waste your time starting up a business that has little chance to survive because you can't possibly deliver the service that you're being paid to provide. If you can't investigate private matters, and do it well, who would be willing to pay you to investigate their confidential, private affairs (other than perhaps your mom, and even then)? So first learn how to investigate civil business, criminal defense, insurance claims, and other private matters before entertaining the idea of starting an investigative agency. You'll spend very little time chasing down criminals; that's what the police do. And PI's don't do what the police do!

How do you learn to investigate private cases? It's a rather simple answer, but a tough pill for some to swallow. You work for someone else that knows how to investigate and is willing to teach you. Schools can only provide you with knowledge. You must be able to apply the knowledge in real life situations. It's called on the job training. You pay the price. You put in your time. You sacrifice to the benefit of someone else that is taking the business and financial risk so that someday someone might sacrifice to your benefit if agency ownership is your goal. You work hard, remain loyal, learn as much as you can, listen to the boss, and stay honest. Your time may eventually come; it may not. If it doesn't, perhaps it wasn't meant to be.

You might find out you're satisfied with field investigation or you don't want the headaches of ownership. It's not all "yellow brick road" and "primrose path" stuff. As I said, it's hard work. But if you want it bad enough, you must be patient. I worked for others for fourteen years (military; security agency; insurance company) before starting my agency. If you let greed get in the way, it'll never happen for you; at least the way I would want it to happen. And don't you dare forget that greed will kill a well-orchestrated intention.

Second, you must have a plan. Almost all business successes are planned. Planning is the cornerstone of organization, order, and success. If you don't have a plan to start and maintain the business, it will not succeed. And the plan must be written down on paper so you can see it, read it, study and memorize it, and show it to others. The official name of the plan in the business world is known as THE BUSINESS PLAN. The business plan is an outline and abstract of how you plan to organize, finance, start, and maintain the business. It sets goals, timelines, and reasonable expectations of success based upon solid business and marketing research; it identifies target markets and maps a marketing strategy, projects income and expense, anticipates growth, and establishes credibility. The business plan defines the purpose, scope, and intent of the business. The plan must be updated and current. In short, you should always have a business plan no matter how successful you think you are or will become. Without it, you have little chance of success. With it, you at least have a chance and an opportunity to get moving. And isn't this what the American dream is all about? Well, you'll have no dream without a plan just as sure as the one who has no plan *without* a dream.

And I'll bet you're wondering: How do I go about outlining and writing a business plan if I've never done it before? And that's the million-dollar question. The answer: You get help. Let me tell you what I did.

I didn't have a clue about business plans. I had no idea how to write one, what one looked like, and didn't even know that I needed one. But I did realize I was a neophyte, at best, in business. Sure, I had dabbled in part time stuff ....plowing in the winter, and running a small food operation at the caddie shack at Worcester Country Club for a summer or two. But I had no real knowledge of how to go about starting a small business that would last until I was ready to retire. So I decided I needed some business training and enrolled in a Worcester Night Life Adult Learning Center ten-week course called "How to Start a Small Business." It's one of the best things I ever did. I had a tremendous classroom teacher in Maryanne Wedgewood of Worcester, MA. She made me realize that starting a small business is to completely alter your lifestyle, forever. I must say that it's true, but you have to experience it yourself because it's different for each person. Maryanne said to all of us "You become the business and the business becomes you." She was right on the money. Maryanne also said, and I'll never let her forget it, "You won't succeed Mr. Lajoie," when I once asked her for something to write with because I had left my pen in the car. Her reasoning was that I was unprepared and one must always be prepared or be prepared to lose out. She really didn't mean I would be a failure, but she said it to drive home a point. In any event, Maryanne taught me everything I needed to know about a business plan. She taught me the basics, gave me the business plan outline, and told me to customize the outline to my particular business idea and then write it myself. She also gave us all sorts of management and business tips, tools, and tricks. We still keep in touch. Maryanne is still teaching people how to start a business. She's had me speak to her students about the road I took, the highs, the lows, and the experiences of going through the start up process. She calls me one of her greatest successes. I am thankful for the knowledge Maryanne imparted to me by way of the Adult Learning Center. I wrote the Lajoie Investigations, Inc. business plan (see Appendix) based upon her teachings.

I also knew I needed to find myself a smart business owner and pick his brain, so I set out to do just that. I found that man by looking no further than a good friend's father, a former accountant for one of the big six accounting firms and a buyer and seller of businesses. Peter Hood, Sr. helped me understand business financing and the financial concerns of starting a small business. Together, we did budgeting and projections. One, three, and five-year financial income and expense projections were done based upon my research and a manageable budget. "Hoodsie" was great! He had the numbers right on the money for the first year and we exceeded the three and five year projections, but not by much. What Pete was doing was projecting slow but successful financial growth to assure the longevity of the business. Every number was based upon reasonable and conservative business estimates and competitive intelligence I had gathered. I then incorporated the projections into my business plan. He wouldn't allow for inflated or embellished numbers. I've adopted his conservative philosophy in this area, and it has served me well. Peter Hood took the time to help me out and he deserves my gratitude and has it. He returned a favor that did not need to be repaid. Only he and a few others will know what I mean. If it wasn't for Peter Hood, I may not have made it. I owe him many thanks. You will need to find someone like him to help you with your projections, your budget, and planning the financial management of your business.

Third, you must execute the business plan as written. What good will a business plan do if you don't follow it? The purpose of a plan is to help guide you in the operation of your business and to present the business proposal to others who are in a position to help you (investors, banks, property managers, providers, and anyone extending credit) I had to present my plan to a bank for a loan. I was terrified. Negative thoughts kept invading my brain: I have no chance...There's no way they'll listen to me...Big bad bank verses young man with a plan...I have no collateral...I'm going nowhere! All I needed was $11,000. So I mustered up the courage to go to the bank with my plan in hand. Let me tell you how it went down.

All my life I had banked with the Worcester County Institution for Savings (WCIS), a local central Massachusetts bank with many branches that eventually got swallowed by Bank of Boston. My parents did their banking there. I had never run into a problem with WCIS. I didn't really know any upper level bank personnel or loan officers at WCIS and they had no major reason to know me. But I needed the money to get going with my plan, establish an office outside of my home in downtown Worcester where all the lawyers are located, and purchase the equipment needed to run the agency. I needed a computer as well. And that may seem routine now, but in 1989 a computer was a big investment. I had never owned a computer. It was the days of the DOS operating system. Computers were for the big boys and the banks.

In any event, I called the main branch of WCIS and spoke to someone in the commercial loan department named Cliff Anderson. I told Cliff that I was planning to start a business and needed a loan to finance the operation. Cliff listened, and then he asked the big question: *"Do you have a business plan?"* Thank God I was ready for him.

I told Cliff not only did I have a plan, but I already had paying clients, financial projections, and an office waiting to be rented. Cliff wanted to set an appointment to meet so I could present the business plan and we could talk about it. I still hadn't mentioned the name of the business or gone into the particulars of my plan. He wanted to meet face to face. An appointment date was set.

I was more than a bit nervous on the day of the appointment. I had to meet Cliff late in the afternoon after I worked a full day at Commerce Insurance Company. I didn't know what to expect or how many other people I'd have to impress. But I knew the plan inside and out. I decided to be up front, cautiously optimistic, and completely truthful (always the best policy). I was dressed business appropriate and clean-shaven. I took a few deep breaths, reminded myself that this was just one bank, and walked into the commercial loan department like the Cowardly Lion was approaching the great and powerful Oz for the first time! This was the moment of truth. And no, I didn't jump through a plate glass window on the way out.

I met Cliff Anderson for the first time. He was not what I expected. It was a first of many meetings in the years ahead. I immediately established a rapport with him because he mentioned that he was Boy Scout leader, just like my father in law; and there were Eagle Scouts in my family. We talked about the Boy Scouts of America, golf, and a few of the same people we both knew. And then we got down to business. The meeting went well. I presented the plan as best I knew how. Cliff showed genuine interest in the investigative profession and agreed that Worcester County was ripe for marketing competent private investigation and information services. He liked the business plan and the fact that my projections were conservative. Cliff was impressed that I already had clients who were providing business and a steady stream of income. I completed the application for a business loan with Cliff's help. I believe I asked for more money than I was seeking in case the bank wanted to chisel the loan amount down. The meeting was in a small office and I felt somewhat claustrophobic, so I was glad to get out. I briefly met Cliff's boss, a loan department VP who was very accommodating and professional. As I was about to leave, Cliff said he'd be in touch and I was on my way. Off I went, just like that. I got into my car and loosened my tie. I sat there for a short time. It was over!

The next day I got a phone call from Cliff and he wanted to know what I was going to put up for collateral. I said, "For a $15,000 three-year term loan at thirteen percent interest?" I guess I wasn't prepared for his question. Cliff said he thought the loan would go through if I put my house up. I was not willing to do it and told him so. I had just bought the house a year before I started the business. There couldn't have been more than $15,000 equity in the house. I just would not do it. I told Cliff I wanted a straight business loan to Lajoie Investigations, Inc. and suggested that a UCC filing where the bank would place a lien on my business property should be sufficient. He then said, "If you're not willing to take any risk, why should we give you the loan? I gotta answer to my boss." I got pissed but held back telling him to go to hell. I said this:

> "My wife is eight months pregnant with our second child and our first child is two and a half years old and you tell me I'm not taking any risk? I just bought a house and a new car and have mortgages to pay and you tell me I'm not taking any risk? I just sunk $10,000 of my own money into the business that came from an employee stock ownership plan I once had with Commerce Insurance Company and you tell me I'm taking

> no risk? I just left a secure job with great benefits and plenty of opportunity to move up and you tell me I'm not willing to take a risk? And on top of all this, I gave up a nice, steady paycheck to go to no guaranteed paycheck and you tell me I'm not willing to take any risk!"

I told Cliff to take my message to his boss and if the boss said no, we would then know who was really willing to take the risk. I also told him there were plenty of banks out there. Cliff was amazed. I'm sure he was shocked. I don't think he expected me to answer in this way. He knew I was upset. Cliff said he'd see what he could do.

Cliff Anderson called me a few days later. I was inside a surveillance van sweating my ass off. I had a big bag cellular phone (remember those dinosaurs?). He told me to find a co-signer and the bank would give me $11,000. I found a person who believed in me...my Dad. Within days I had an unsecured loan debt to add to my pressures and stress level. I had to bank heavily on my business plan to see me through the tough beginnings. Cliff kept track of me throughout the three year loan repayment period. He cared. I did more business with him and WCIS. They were good to me. I never missed a loan payment. Years later, Cliff told me it was my business plan that impressed him and attracted the attention of his boss. He also told me the fact that I executed my plan as written was a major reason as to why my business is successful and thriving.

I'll tell you one thing; a business plan *must* be followed. If your plan is sound, reasonable, and every effort is made to follow it, it will only be a matter of time before the business becomes successful. No doubt there will be times when you must veer from it due to unforeseen circumstances, but don't stray too far off course. Amend the plan to adapt and deal with these circumstances, especially in the infancy of the business. But always stick to the core principles in your plan. I know I did and the results were remarkable and rewarding. And I still reap the spoils of my business plan to this day.

Fourth, you must work hard. If you think you're going to sit back after you've established the business, obtained a business loan, set up the office, hung out your shingle, and then wait for the clients and money to start rolling on in, you are delusional and most definitely mistaken. Nothing, and I mean nothing, comes to you without hard work. Blood, sweat, and tears are mandatory. Ninety-hour weeks are commonplace. In the beginning, you rarely have time to see your family. It's true of starting any business. Your life is the business. The business is your life. And business is business.

What about law enforcement officers who are getting ready to retire and contemplate private investigation as a source of income? For years, law enforcement officers have protected the public against criminals, conducted criminal investigations for the prosecution, and have worked to assure the safety of citizens. They put their lives on the line each and every day as peace officers. For that I am grateful and commend them for their service. It's a tough job for sure and they have my unmitigated respect. Most ex law enforcement, however, think they are much more qualified to conduct private investigation than those who have no law enforcement experience. I have news for those that think like this – nothing could be further from the truth! Some ex-law enforcement officers also think it's a right of passage to become licensed as a PI; they then think the private work will come rushing in. It doesn't work that way! Just because someone becomes licensed as a PI and that someone is ex law enforcement, it doesn't mean he or she is any more entitled to clientele than a person aspiring to be a PI who has no law enforcement background. It has been my experience that some law enforcement officers, as well some of the ones with no law enforcement background, who eventually become PI's work only hard enough to become marginally successful within the PI profession. Then they complain incessantly and become extremely jealous of those PI's that are successful. Let's try to avoid this if we can in order to co-exist in peace. Listen up: If you are considering the PI profession, work hard and learn how to investigate civil, criminal defense, and insurance claims matters *before* you hang out your shingle. Your time as a police officer, FBI or Treasury agent, military investigator, state trooper, corrections officer, insurance investigator, legal investigator, DSS investigator, and so forth gives you no special right as a PI or a magic wand to solve private cases. In fact, it may hinder your effectiveness as a PI. If you are law enforcement (or anyone else for that matter but especially law enforcement) and are considering a career as a PI, ask yourself if you can investigate for the accused murderer; work for the alleged child rapist; investigate police officer misconduct; obtain information without the use of a badge and uniform; conduct complex commercial liability insurance coverage investigation; interview and obtain recorded statements of children involved in a detailed domestic custody dispute; and I could go on and on and on. Ask yourself if you will work hard to assure the rights of the accused and protect the interests of attorneys, corporations, private parties, and insurance companies. If you're not sure, please do yourself a favor and retire, or find yourself another line of work if you must work. But if you can get by the moral issue of whose interest you must protect, go work hard for an existing PI agency, insurance company, or private entity willing to train you. You already have basic investigative training and should know the fundamentals of investigation. You now need to learn to apply the principles of what you already know to investigation involving the private sector. It's a completely different animal than what a law enforcement officer is used to- working for the public to serve and protect. But it can be done if you work hard and are willing to commit to retraining. You will still be able to serve and protect; it's just that the private, paying client will be the one you serve and protect in a different sort of way. And please do not try to hang up a shingle without obtaining a PI license and/or a business license if it is required (required in almost all fifty states). You have no right or any special privileges, so let's try to play by the same rules.

One of my best friends is an ex-OSI (USAF) and was a narcotics officer with the Orlando Police Department. Kerry Farney, CLI, started his business about the same time I started mine. I didn't befriend him until about ten years ago. We happened to meet because we both became members of the National Association of Legal Investigators (NALI) in the early 1990's and attended the same NALI continuing education functions. We both have a strong work ethic that was partly the result of our training in the USAF. Kerry made a successful transition from law enforcement because he worked hard and trained to learn the elements of private sector investigation. His transition was smooth but by no means easy. Kerry is an expert in DUI investigation and frequently lectures about DUI criminal defense investigation at trade and association seminars around the country. He has worked for high profile, famed attorney Geoffrey Fieger; Kerry worked the Dr. Kevorkian homicide cases when Fieger was Kevorkian's attorney. Kerry is now considered one of the top private investigators in the country. He and I routinely work cases together. We compliment each other well. I have no law enforcement experience and he does, but we both respect each other's past work history and investigative acumen. We have a lot in common and it's kind of scary how we both think alike concerning private investigation matters. It's amazing what can be accomplished when two hard working PI's put their experience and intelligence together on a case file. And he and I will both attest to the mind-boggling cases we have successfully worked and worked hard. The results are always awe-inspiring. Of course, the clients become the ultimate beneficiaries of the successes; but so are we because we compliment each other, help each other look good, and promote PI teamwork. Teaming (a difficult concept most PI's struggle to understand) with another competent PI to strengthen the investigation for the client is always in the best interest of the profession and the client. Don't forget it.

There are other top PI's who were law enforcement officers before entering the PI world; my friends Rory McMahon, Ellis Armistead, Julius "Buddy" Bombet, and Warren Sonne are successful, extremely competent PI's. They have worked hard to make the transition to the private sector. There are many others in the PI profession who have nothing but law enforcement background and are successful. There are also many people in the PI profession who don't have one iota of law enforcement experience and are top-notch professional private investigators. The common denominator with good, solid, successful PI's is hard work, intelligence, and PI training and continuing education; not just a law enforcement or criminal justice background; or not just insurance SIU and casualty claim experience.

So no matter where you come from, you can get to where you want to be through good old-fashioned hard work. And if you're not there yet, keep working hard because it's good for business. And business is business.

Fifth, you must have good business sense. I can't even begin to estimate the number of PI's that have little or no business sense, but I know there are many. They might be tremendous case file investigators in the field but have a hard time in the office, or managing people. To own a successful agency with employees, you must have good business acumen. This does not mean you need an MBA from Harvard, or even a business degree, to run a PI agency. I don't have either one although the MBA from Harvard sounds enticing. But I'm good at running the business, i.e....marketing, negotiating, business problem solving, delegating, keeping good employees, and knowing when I'm in over my head. You might say I understand my limitations. Most of this stuff is common sense, but for some esoteric reason the business of private investigation oftentimes turns the great common sense PI into an unemployed PI. It could be as easy to solve as increasing ones hourly rates or collecting accounts receivables. It might be that field investigators cannot balance the business work with the investigation work. Pay too much attention to one and the other suffers. The owner of an agency must strike a balance. The more employees you have, the less time you will spend out in the field, and vice versa. And finding the *right* balance is certainly a key element in running a successful private investigation business. It's different for each owner. I spend much less time in the field now than I did in 1990, or even in 2002. My business is growing. I have more employees. But potential owners beware: never, ever, stop investigating. Once an owner stops rolling up the sleeves, employee investigators lose some degree of respect for the owner. I always have five to ten active cases and spend about twenty to thirty hours a week working those cases, sometimes many more. These cases are the big ones, the cases nobody else in the agency wants or can't yet do, or the ones I take a specific interest in working: high profile murders; sex crimes; wrongful death actions; catastrophic injury cases; complex insurance coverage matters, missing persons, and the like. I wouldn't ask one of my employees to do something I wouldn't do or haven't done. And that's good business. And business is business.

Remember; do not mix business and family, business and pleasure, and business and friendship without knowing exactly what you're doing because it can be fatal. Have confidence in yourself and work and train hard. Have a solid business plan and be prepared for the unexpected. Be willing to make sacrifices, roll with the punches, and know your limitations. Be fair with yourself and others. Promote teamwork and be professional.

I know I've made it sound as if starting and maintaining a private investigation business is nearly next to impossible. And though it's not impossible, it's not easy either. It is within grasp, especially if you use good business sense and work hard. Don't forget that you can always purchase an existing agency as well. Many PI's have succeeded as attested by the thousands of successful agencies in the USA and around the world. You, too, can own an agency, start a PI business, and thrive, but it's not for everyone. Follow your dreams but be realistic, because, you guessed it... business is business.

6
SUCCESS & FAILURE

Always bear in mind that your own resolution to succeed is more important than any one thing.

Abraham Lincoln

Success means different things to different people. Certainly, the degree of success a business or individual achieves varies from one person to the next. What one person views as successful may be a failure to the next person and vice versa. That's because the standard of measuring success is usually an opinion, based upon values, wants, and needs, rather than a set definition. For instance, most people view money and financial status as the ultimate measurement of success; those that do usually reason if a business or individual is flush with money then they must be successful. Happiness is another standard by which some measure success. Again, the reasoning here is that if a person is happy, then he/she must be successful. And there are many standards and opinions out there depending upon the individual making an assessment of success based on their value system. Truth be told, however, it may be that the wealthy and the happy ones are not too successful. So let's flush the value assessment of success right down the toilet. Trust me; it's the right thing to do!

Rather than to set standards for measuring success, I believe each person should define success individually, set goals, and seek to achieve them. Simply put, I define success as obtaining a desired result of a set goal. If you have no goal, you cannot succeed because you can't possibly know where success begins or where it ends. Some people set their goals too high, and they never realize a success. And some people set goals low so they experience a lot of small successes. But are they operating at their optimum potential? Most times, no. Some people do not set goals at all but rather decide to do something until they are satisfied. I guess that's okay but we're right back to trying to determine where the success starts and ends.

You must first establish goals to realize success or failure. Your personal and business goals should be reasonable and attainable. Only you truly know your talents, limitations, and shortcomings. Base your goals on knowledge of yourself, your ambition, and your reasonable desires. For instance, if you plan to live in a house rather than live in an apartment, set the goal of purchasing a house based upon income, savings, and a reasonable time period to purchase. If you plan to start a business, set the goal of establishing the business by a certain time based upon reasonable expectations and a sound business plan (we talked about the business plan earlier). Each and every goal you set should have a definite time period in which you strive to attain the goal. It's called a deadline.

Having no set deadline to reach a goal also means you cannot adequately evaluate success, or, for that matter, failure. If you're happy and satisfied not knowing how you stack up with others doing the same thing, then don't set deadlines. If it takes you your entire life to learn how to tie your shoes, you might have reached the set goal, but is this considered a success? You decide.

So let's talk about setting deadlines because deadlines are important in business, as they are in your personal life. Deadlines are a fact of everyday life in the PI world. There are deadlines on every case assignment, sometimes a number of them on each case.

Don't meet the deadline and you might lose a client. When you're starting out and a client has to have those records by a certain point in time and you fail to produce the records by the deadline date, do you think this client will be inclined to assign another investigation, particularly if the client has deadlines that need to be met? Probably not.

In almost all cases involving legal investigation (investigation of matters for lawyers who might eventually file lawsuits), there must be established goals for the successful completion of a case based upon deadlines. These lawyers have deadlines themselves. Most civil cases are fast-tracked (court imposed deadlines). Criminal cases afford the defendant the right to a speedy trial unless that right is waived. There is this phase of any civil and criminal case called discovery. Discovery is when the parties of the litigation make disclosures and release information to each other about their case. The most common forms of discovery are production of documents; release of exculpatory information; interrogatories; depositions (remember the "bull fighter" story); offers of proof. The bottom line is that discovery is date sensitive. So when a lawyer calls upon a PI to conduct investigation by a certain date, unless there is an extension, you had better have it done by that date. If you are assigned a locate investigation by an insurance company to locate the defendant because interrogatories (a set of questions propounded by the opposing side of a lawsuit) are due in... let's say... seven days, you had better locate the defendant pronto so that the interrogatories can be completed, signed, and filed in court before the deadline. If it's late, you have failed the goal. If you find the defendant and communicate it to the client before *your own* deadline, and not the court's, success is assured.

There are a million other examples of investigative deadlines I could cite. Most are boring but necessary. SIU deadlines are some of the most demanding deadlines in insurance defense investigation (PI's want to have insurance companies as clients because they have lots of investigations to assign and it's steady, long term income). SIU (Special Investigation Unit) investigations are insurance investigations involving the theft of motor vehicles, staged accidents, operator and garaging matters, jump-ins, build up cases, and any investigation relating to potential insurance fraud. These investigations are typically customer service oriented because most of the time they involve the policy holder (the insured). The insured pays the company a premium and is the customer. The company and the insured are bound by an insurance contract called a policy. There are statutes, case law, and plenty of mandated regulations that stem from an insurance policy guiding and governing the insurance adjusting of a claim. When an incident occurs, claims must be investigated thoroughly and a decision on payment made promptly. Most companies have ten, fifteen, twenty five, and thirty day report deadlines depending on the type and scope of the investigation. You are judged upon the quality of the investigation but also upon your compliance with the reporting deadlines. You could be the most productive SIU investigative vendor for the top insurer in your state, but if you're habitually late on mandatory deadlines, what does that say about the customer service aspect of your investigations? And what message are you sending to the insurance company? It's not the right message – that's for sure! Insurance companies are difficult to land as clients and you don't want to continually answer phone calls from the adjusters screaming, "Where is my report?" If deadlines are not met, they'll find someone who can meet them and you'll be history. Now that's *not* a success story by any stretch of the imagination.

The importance of deadlines is immense, especially in insurance investigation. Here's a true story about a rather important deadline that resulted in a failure. In the early 1990's, my agency was assigned an important and sensitive surveillance on a large loss case by a relatively new insurance company client involving a claimant who alleged he couldn't perform physical activity involving the cutting of wood. A surveillance investigator was assigned to the case and conducted surveillance of the claimant for several days each week for a month or so. Somehow, I lost track of the case, the reason which now escapes me. The investigator assigned to the case had obtained video of the claimant chopping wood for several hours each week; it was good solid evidence. The agency never submitted a report or invoice for about eight days of surveillance, roughly four thousand dollars worth of work. The investigator let the deadline slide by about two months, and we also missed it administratively. I realized what was happening when the adjuster called me asking if we could submit a report and invoice (*Where's my report!)* because the case had settled for the policy limit. The adjuster commented something to the effect that they could have settled the case for short money if we could have obtained video of the claimant chopping wood. He assumed we didn't have anything they could use because we had not yet submitted a report. I nearly had a heart attack right then and there. I had to tell the adjuster what we had because he was asking for a report. There was a deafening silence at the end of the telephone line. The adjuster then said, "Better not send the report OR the invoice." I've never heard from that insurance company adjuster again (and probably never will). I lost roughly four grand and a client. Hard lesson learned all because of a missed deadline. What a huge failure. Since then we've never failed a case or client because we missed a deadline, and checks and balances have been instituted to prevent such a reoccurrence. What happened to the investigator, you might wonder? Let's just say he didn't last too long after this fiasco. But it was ultimately my responsibility – I paid the price. *Mess up, fess up!*

Enough negative talk about deadlines. You get the point. Establish your case investigation goals by setting deadlines and meeting them. Get the job done within the allotted time and the investigation will be successful if due diligence in quality was maintained.

The results of an investigation do not determine whether the case investigation was a success or a failure. No investigator can guaranty the results of any investigation prior to the investigation taking place – it's ludicrous to think otherwise. A professional investigator can only guaranty that he or she will provide their best investigative efforts. Some clients want investigators to believe that an investigation is not successful if the desired facts *they* want aren't revealed. What's there is there. No one can change the facts of any incident, accident, crime, or occurrence. If an investigation reveals all the true facts in the time allotted to conduct the investigation and reach established goals, it's a successful investigation. If an investigation doesn't reveal all the facts but just enough true facts to help the client obtain a desired end result, it's a successful investigation. If a criminal investigation reveals true facts that inculpates the defendant, so be it; it's a successful investigation. The attorney client will then know to plead the case. No case investigation needs to reveal every fact because a lot of the circumstances surrounding an incident are not relevant. No one person can know everything about everything on a matter requiring an investigation. Most clients want an investigator to stay focused on the relevant facts, as does the professional investigator himself. For example, the color of a car isn't usually relevant when trying to determine civil liability of an auto accident, but it might be useful to know in a criminal case of leaving the scene of a personal injury accident. The pocketknife a homicide victim was carrying is really not relevant unless the knife was pulled just before or during the incident. Focusing on irrelevant issues leads to an investigation breakdown and can turn a successful investigation into a failure.

A professional investigator lets no client run an investigation. I run from these clients if they try. Although they are paying the freight, clients only pay for an investigator's time and attention to detail. They are not paying for puppetry. A PI should never grovel to any attorney or bootlick any insurance adjuster when ethics and principles are being stretched beyond the limit because no matter what anyone does or says, the investigation will be a complete failure. Do not allow the client to micro-manage the investigation. Some clients will think they own you once they've given you a case assignment, especially the private ones. But the worst ones are the new insurance adjusters assigning surveillances who feel they must tell you when to come and go from a claimant's house and how to conduct the investigation; especially the ones who were private investigators before they ended up leaving the PI business. And they know better.

I can recall an adjuster sending us a list of instructions almost two pages long outlining an entire surveillance investigation and then some – what days and times to do the surveillance, what kind of camera to use in different situations, what to do in the event we saw the claimant, how to make contact with the claimant when a face to face pretext was necessary, what to do in the event we got burned, and even what kind of report to write. This adjuster was a control freak. But the worst of it was the adjuster said he wanted us to get *good* video of the claimant engaged in some "healthy activity." When I read the instructions, I wanted to puke. So I called the adjuster to ask what we should do in the event the claimant is observed in some "unhealthy activity." Big mistake. I was on the phone with this jerk for over thirty minutes. Once I realized there was never going to be any way to satisfy this guy, I politely refused the case. Then I told him not to call my office again to assign a case if he didn't trust us. And trust looms large with me. A PI's job is to document *all* activity of a claimant during the times the claimant is observed. It is not dependent on whether or not the claimant's activity is "healthy" or "unhealthy," whatever that means. Do not compromise your ethics and values for money. It's just not worth it. During surveillance, any surveillance, PI's observe and document the activities and the conduct of the subject, nothing more, nothing less. If you're an insurance adjuster or investigator, please try not to make surveillance something it isn't. And do not call a PI who has conducted surveillance at your instruction to complain that he or she "*didn't get*" what you wanted. It is what it is......please realize it may take more time to determine a claimant's activity level. More time means you need to invest more money. I have kept statistics over the years showing the more time an adjuster allows to conduct surveillance, the better chance of obtaining evaluative video of a subject. The statistics conclude that one day surveillances are typically a waste of money. Two and three day surveillances are the best value. And multiple day surveillances over long periods of time are extremely valuable and cost effective.

Those investigators that let the client attempt to control the outcome of an investigation have failed the client, themselves, and the profession. And I'm loath to say there's a few of those PI types out there. Money should not be the supreme motivating factor, although I would be lying if I said it wasn't important. Money is important because every investigator needs to be paid. But if a PI conducts successful investigations, the money will eventually come. There's nothing like word of mouth advertising for the successful investigator by attorneys and insurance adjusters. Of course, the caveat is it can work in reverse as well for the investigator who has failed the client. Let's not go there.

Respect is a word that is used a lot and it just might be the most misunderstood word in the English dictionary. People kill people over what they think are respect issues. Ever heard a person say "He disrespected me" when asked why they bludgeoned a knife into someone's heart? I have. It's prevalent in gang related homicide. Rodney Dangerfield (God rest his comic soul) made the phrase "I don't get no respect" famous. *Respect*......It really didn't bother Dangerfield one way or the other; or if it did, he never let the world know it. Why? Easy answer; Dangerfield *was* respected by others but he wanted his audience to believe he wasn't because it was a part of his routine.

And, of course, you hear sports superstar's use the word "respect" incessantly as if it were theirs alone. Most big time sports players who use respect in contract negotiations (usually done through the press and other media outlets) think respect means money, money, and more money. Respect has *nothing* to do with money. If it did, my wallet would be a lot fatter. It has to do with setting a positive example, appropriate manners and civility, character, and treating others with dignity. And you can't buy that with any amount of money.

Everyone wants to be respected: to be held in high honor; to be given admirable consideration by your fellow man; to be regarded with great esteem; to be revered; to treat someone with deference; to be acknowledged and recognized by your peers in a positive way.

Respect – it don't come easy. It must be earned. Period! There are no if, ands, or buts about earning respect. Why would any general manager give in to a sports star's money demands based on a false or misunderstood use of the word respect? Why should anyone, including a rival gang member, respect another gang member when the respect is based upon fear and not honor or esteem? Someone said there is an honor amongst thieves. Whoever said it was out of his mind. There is never any honor in criminal behavior...so how can there be respect? There can't be.

There are four groups that a PI must respect to be considered successful.

PI's must respect other PI's who have earned the respect and are due recognition. PI's are a different breed when it comes time to dole out due respect, acknowledgement, and recognition, especially when it comes to a competing PI. Ego usually gets in the way and jealousy takes over. There are many PI's who view successful PI's who have been locally and nationally recognized with scorn, contempt, outrage, or quiet objection. Why? Ego is the answer. They reason "I'm the best" and think it should be them gaining the respect and recognition. I say the more PI's that are respected by acknowledgement and recognition, as long as it's earned and due, the better for every PI and the profession. It's getting better because associations and PI leaders are carrying the torch to set the example, but it's far from perfect. Just about the worst thing a PI can do is to seek out recognition for himself. When one seeks recognition and it comes, it's worthless. When one doesn't seek it and it comes, it's priceless! Showing respect to other deserving PI's is to show character and friendship. Work hard and earn the respect of your bother and sister PI's. It's extremely satisfying and you can take it from someone who knows both sides of the coin. `Nuff said.

PI's must show respect to clients. I shouldn't have to explain this one. Clients have earned the respect simply because of the position they hold. They are the "customer." Can you imagine disrespecting your customer? If you want to survive in the PI world, respect to the client is automatic unless they fall into disrespect. If so, you have a decision to make and it might not be an easy one as economics may enter the decision-making processes. For me, the decision is easy. For you, who knows, but you probably know what I would say. Respecting clients will breed success.

PI's must show respect to their employees. If you become lucky enough to employ people, treat them as you would like to be treated by others. Treat your employees with disrespect and they will quickly disappear. This does not mean be a nice guy all the time instead of a boss. It does mean being thoughtful and fair, professional and business minded. Your employees are not your property so don't treat them as such. Do not, under any circumstance, talk down or patronize your employees.

A hard and true worker will gain respect quickly from a PI manager or agency owner. Make sure you don't take advantage of any employee. Get rid of the ones who are stale and unproductive. The good employees will appreciate it and respect the decision. When recognition is due an employee, acknowledge him or her in front of all employees. When an employee needs to be admonished, do it in private. Respect your employees and you'll realize much more than success. They will come to respect and admire you. You will be a true leader.

PI's must show respect to Law Enforcement. Contrary to what some PI's actually believe, and have even published, law enforcement is not the enemy. How do you expect to obtain cooperation from police, police record clerks, corrections officers, DA's, and the local sheriff's office if you disrespect and/or hold some sort of grudge against them? You'll be dealing with these people all the time. If you treat law enforcement personnel as if they were second-class citizens by insulting their dignity, they will probably ignore you or, more likely, you'll have trouble. You will find it difficult to do your job if they believe you're making it difficult for them to do theirs. It's really simple. Treat law enforcement as you want to be treated – with professional respect. They have a job to do and it's a tough, dangerous job. The sooner you realize it, the better. And be forewarned, law enforcement officers are not going to trust you right away. Conversely, you don't have to trust law enforcement right away either. Trust must be earned. Police detectives and private investigators are working their sides in some criminal matter, auto accident, or civil situation. So be civil! *Both* PI's and police should be loyal to their employer and look to protect their interests. *Both* should be cautious when dealing with each other because there is a duty to do so. To do otherwise would be foolish. Please, though, for the sake of professionalism and reputation, be respectful and remain dignified. Even though there'll be times it may seem like it, it is not an "us and them" mentality for most law enforcement personnel or private sector investigators. So don't you try to make it that way. Try to understand each other's position and limitations. Try to find a common ground that might allow you to be helpful to each other. It'll pay off in the long run.

Of course, there are many more groups and people who deserve respect, but disrespect PI's, clients, employees, and law enforcement and you most certainly will fail. About the only good thing that can come out of this is you probably won't be killed, but you never know. You should treat all people with dignity and respect until there is reason to void the respect. Human decency calls for respectful relationships. Respectful relationships foster goodwill. Goodwill and respect, along with hard work, will produce success.

Setting goals, meeting deadlines, maintaining quality in work, and cultivating respectful relations will lead to success in any business. In the PI world, finding success is no different. No matter what you do, there will be successes and failures. And, of course, the main goal is to try to experience more success than failure. But the beauty of life is that if you fall, you can pick yourself right back up and start all over again. Don't quit if it happens to you. Quitters fail. Winners succeed. Success is not intangible if you have attainable goals. Write them down and follow your dreams with conviction. If you don't take a chance on your dreams, you'll be left wondering for the rest of your life, what if? For the sake of success, it's much better to say "why not!"

7
SECOND FIDDLE

But if the good people, in their wisdom, shall see fit to keep me in the background, I have been too familiar with disappointment to be very much chagrined.

Abraham Lincoln

It took me a long time to get to the point when being disappointed by people, places, and things did not matter much anymore. Disappointments are a fact of life, although I wish they weren't. Failures, let-downs, breaches of trust, malfunction, frustration, catastrophes, tragedy, untruthfulness, incompetence, fiasco's, tirades, jealousy, and disloyalty are what we all deal with on a daily basis, some more than others. These descriptors, and others to be sure, all cause some level of disappointment. The degree of disappointment depends solely upon the affected individual. Because of my career experiences, I can now say with some level of confidence that private investigators endure many more disappointments than does the average American worker in the course of an eight-hour workday. The word "NO" is routinely the norm when PI's request some public record. Lack of respect and jealously is oftentimes encountered when PI's try to work with or obtain information from law enforcement (especially if the PI is *not* former law enforcement). Employee dishonesty can be the bane of existence if it hits your agency. Lack of training and education can be troublesome in this profession. I could go on and on with examples of situations that will cause disappointment to the professional private investigator. It's somewhat depressing.

And nothing disappoints most people more than having to play "second fiddle." It's certainly no different in the investigative profession. "Second fiddle" has different meanings to different people. To the disgruntled PI or employee, "second fiddle" is how they negatively interpret their position in the agency. For example, and I quote: "I do most of the work and get no credit;" "I deserve this case, but I always lose out to someone else;" "how come I don't get considered for a position in the agency when I'm the obvious choice;" "I'm not being recognized when I deserve the academy award;" "I'm being stepped on when I should be stepped up;" "they'd be nothing without me." I suppose it's the same in most industries. But it's certainly prevalent in the private investigation profession where jealousy and self-serving interests grow like mold in a warm, moist environment. Most PI's want to be the top dog, make all the decisions, control everything; be the man. And that's never OK, not even if you own the agency. I'm loath to admit that the private investigation profession, for the most part, is greed and ego driven. It's one of the main reasons why most PI agencies have one, maybe two, investigators, and are limited in growth potential. And the agencies that employ more than two people find it increasingly difficult to keep top notch, loyal employees because of it. Many PI's think they are the best this business has to offer; in reality, it's usually the opposite and most have much to learn. I've experienced these types who worked at my agency over the past fifteen years and are now former employees. They started out like gang busters and eventually turn critical when things didn't go their way; then they whined like babies and badmouthed me when I wasn't around. For the record, they weren't fooling anyone, only themselves. So I've determined that "second fiddle" is an esoteric truism many PI's are unable to accept, much less comprehend.

I have a different definition of "second fiddle." Although not easy to deal with, "second fiddle" is doing your job by making your boss or the client look good. And in order to survive in this business (or any business), you must learn to cope with it most of the time. "Second fiddle" may be the way of life at your agency, in your associations, and when you're working investigations. In almost all cases, a PI will be "second fiddle" to the agency owner and to the client, especially if the clients are attorneys or corporate types. I can speak from experience: "second fiddle" is no fun, especially when it doesn't seem fair. More times than not, a private investigator is a case-maker or a case-breaker. It is an attorney that usually delivers that case making or breaking information, almost always reaping the rewards of the outcome and the glory that might come with it. Keep in mind that the attorney will suffer the consequences from failure if the case goes bad. Sometimes, the PI feels the heat. Ultimately, the private investigator must determine if fame and glory is something that really matters. If it matters, you might want to try another profession. Incredible liability and financial risks, confidentiality issues, and the tremendous responsibilities that agency owners tolerate daily, twenty four - seven, do not make fame and glory a laudable goal.

Despite agency ownership, owners *always* play "second fiddle," especially to the people that pay the bills and the invoices - the clients. Truth be told, it's no picnic in the park to be the owner of an agency but it does have its rewards if the employees are honest and loyal.

Let's forget about me. It's you I'm talking to, whether or not you are the employee or potential employee of a professional PI agency, or an employee of any company, "second fiddle" is something you *must* accept with grace and learn how to manage to a point where you and your boss are happy or at least satisfied. Most people cannot do it. If you are the one that can, you'll most likely do well and success will come that much easier. If you're the "know-it-all" type, the one that cannot accept constructive criticism, the person that can't easily let clients or bosses take credit for something you did in the normal course of your employment, then seek counseling if you plan to stay in the business of professional private investigation or, for that matter, any business. Check your ego in at the door or at least have control of it. Because if you don't, "second fiddle" can surely do you in, in more ways than you'll ever want to know or find out.

I deal with "second fiddle" fairly well now but there was a time when I did not. Live and learn. Now, I consider payment for services rendered as my thanks and praise for a job well done. If a pat on the back or some bit of glory accompanies the money, then great. But I don't go looking for praise, glory, thanks, or the like. If it comes to me, I'm grateful, but I don't hold my breath waiting for it. If I did, I'd be dead many times over. If you are able to accept "second fiddle" and simultaneously remain humble and true, your time will come. And when it does, it will be that much sweeter.

If you are unable to control your ego, you'll be squeezed out of the PI profession at some point. If you try to control people and events, you'll end up being controlled by other forces; forces you will neither like nor accept. Bosses, supervisors, managers, and clients all have one thing in common: they call the shots. No boss likes to be intentionally shown-up or screwed by a disgruntled employee who can't be a good "second fiddle." Remember, when decisions are being made by people trusted with positions of power, they expect the employee to be a "second fiddle" player. The work product that you provide to make people like me look good is rewarded by a paycheck and a pat on the back. Anything else that comes along with it is simply a bonus. Employees are supposed to make their bosses look good. Agency owners are supposed to make the clients look good. If you can play the "second fiddle" fairly well over an extended period of time, you just might find yourself the conductor some day. If not, you'll be the understudy for the rest of your life.

8
PERSONALITIES

I don't think much of a man who is not wiser today than he was yesterday.

Abraham Lincoln

I have met, experienced, employed, confronted, developed friendships, disliked, and loved a lot of people during my time as a professional private investigator and a member of the human race, both inside and outside the profession; each one different and distinct in some natural, or unnatural, way. And so have you unless you've been hiding under a rock all your life. I'm sure you've figured out that there are many, many personality types and many variations of different personalities. In life, you will meet and greet all kinds of people. And the same holds true in the PI world. I am by no means a professional psychologist, sociologist, or anthropologist; I do, however, know a little something about people and have an instinctive talent to pick up on personalities almost immediately. Accurately assessing personalities is not an easy task, but it's something you must do and do well each and every day to survive in the PI world.

What follows is a sampling of the personality types I believe you need to hear about. Personality is the cornerstone by which you and other people are viewed and judged. And that's important. It's important to know your personality type or types. And yes, you can have multiple personality traits. But it's more important to know the personality traits of those people you will deal with as a PI.

When I was a young child until I was in my early twenties, I didn't know private investigators existed! The occupation was a mystery to me. I'm not one of those people who knew what they wanted to be in life at time of birth or from the moment of conception. And to tell you the truth, I have a problem with these types anyway... not only do I not believe most of them, I have found that they are workaholics for the most part. And boy are they BORING! The cliché "all work and no play makes for a boring person" is absolutely true. And they sometimes turn into control freaks that believe they are in absolute control. Of course, more times than not they are out of control, which in and of itself creates a myriad of other problems. They never admit they are wrong and are loath to apologize for a mistake. I call this personality type "The Speedo." They make horrible private investigators, even worse clients, and are usually unhappy people. If you are "the Speedo", I suggest a career as an administrative executive in corporate America or try your luck as a widget auditor for a manufacturing facility. But do not consider the profession of private investigation...please.

Then there are many people who are happy to live a life where mediocrity and stupidity mesh to create the person that I refer to as "The Magoo." They haven't got a clue and really don't care except when it's time for a raise in pay or a job review. They are usually self-centered and rely on others to pull their weight. Many times they look busy but accomplish nothing. Production and organization are not words they understand; they even have a hard time locating them in the dictionary. They leave work early, come in late, and are (allegedly) sick a lot. Excuses are plentiful with this type. And they'll "yes" you to death when given direction or constructive criticism. They make tons of personal phone calls which they believe a sacred right and are always planning vacations, family gatherings, shopping spree's, ...anything but work. Although I like to plan vacations and frequently do (I'll get to that later), I do not recommend doing it during work hours. These people could never survive as private investigators unless, of course, they are receiving rather large pensions, but they make great clients. If you look in the mirror and see "the Magoo," you might want to consider menial work in some municipal, state, or federal government agency.

There is a personality type in the world known to me as "The Sycophant." This animal is a flattering social butterfly one moment and a cold hearted back stabber the next. He/she is almost always disingenuous, self aggrandizing, and looking for favors. They spread rumors, lack honesty, and will step all over someone else just to get ahead. Although they are usually hard workers, there is always a personal ulterior motive that is a subterfuge for their efforts. Brown nosing is such a way of life with these types, it turns diplomacy into a one sided joke. Watch out for the guy who'll sell you out to gain an edge, because it is the Sycophant doing what he does best. Most pathological liars and con artists are sycophants. They may even be criminals. They are very good at doing what they do best as described above, so you might never know it. They get ahead at the expense of others and can absolutely NOT be relied upon or trusted. Their loyalty is to no person but themselves. Unfortunately, there are more sycophants than you might think in the private investigation profession, but they are by no means professional. They're the ones that give PI's a bad name, break the laws and trash ethics, look for the press, blame others for the failures of their own making, and get ahead at the expense of you and me. I have no use for sycophants. If you hang out with these types, you might eventually become one of them. Although they may have money to spend on investigation, they make for difficult clients. I run from them. And so should you.

"The Pinocchio" is - you guessed it - a liar. Some are pathological liars and some are deceptive liars. I run into these types a lot. Pathological liars lie so much and to such a deep extent that they even begin to believe their own lies. Once they tell a lie they need another one to cover it up. The lies snowball and are easy to pick out. Deceptive liars lie by peppering truths with lies. Deceptive liars try to avoid detection of their own deceit. They are hard to pick out and almost never admit to a lie. Pinocchio's are usually control freaks but are never in control; they only think they are. What's truly sad is they usually end up devastating lives and disappointing people at work and at home. These types think they have all the answers, never admit they are wrong, and think they are better than all others. It's either their way or the highway; there's no in between. Some are criminals, but most are not or just haven't been caught. They certainly like being vain and telling the world about it. Unfortunately, Pinocchio's are drawn to the investigation field. It's too bad and I'm somewhat ashamed to admit it. But keep in mind there are these types in every field. Pinocchio's never make great clients but frequently need investigation, especially in criminal defense cases, so they are a good source of income. I say let them pay for their lies!

The "Lazy Hangman" is one who will start working gangbusters when newly hired and then fade into lazy oblivion three months to a year down the road. At first, they work just hard enough to make it past the probation period. After they have their raise and benefits secured, it's only a matter of short time before they rear their ugly work habits. They eventually hang themselves with their own noose when the boss is at wits end and co-employees are ready to kill them (and the boss). Most live in low-income apartments, watch TV for hours on end, and treat their kids as if they were slaves. Some are drawn to prescription medication for perceived medical problems. Their intelligence level is suspect. Most cannot be trusted and make up little white lies to avoid blame. They drain the company coffers, are a financial liability, and are more likely than not to commit employee theft. They take credit for work that others do and will steal the thunder from those who try to help them. The "Lazy Hangman" is susceptible to drug addiction and criminal behavior. They are inclined to file questionable insurance claims and lawsuits when involved in an accident, incident, or a dispute. And even though they are a great source of income for PI's and attorneys, avoid employing them at all costs. If you have a few of these types working for you now, make sure you don't hang onto to them too long or they'll end up hanging you.

Another type of personality is one I call "The Bus Rider," a good, devote, and honest person who wants nothing more than to live a happy and content life without major problems. They are usually not great decision makers and don't want to be. For the most part, they can solve problems but complex thinking is not what they excel in. They usually panic in an immediate problem or emergency situation. Nevertheless, they are fiercely loyal and, when given a task, will go to all ends during work hours to accomplish their mission. Most are extremely competent and efficient and can be counted on to get the job done. They are never late, will work overtime as long as they are paid, and own small homes. They are definitely cost conscious, sometimes cheap. They make wonderful parents, show up at every school and athletic function, and vote in every election. They are the foot soldier of a modern society and make up the majority of the work force. The Bus Rider can be a good, competent private investigator under the direction of others above him or her. There is no doubt in my mind that they make the best clients and set the example for other potential Bus Riders to follow. Never turn them away as clients because they are simply good people who may need help from time to time and someone to turn to in times of need. They are not too hard to satisfy, but never take advantage of them. They do not forget.

Last but certainly not least is "The Professional." And I'm fortunate to be able to say that there are many of these types out there who become excellent clients and good sources of income. They are intelligent and witty. They are also demanding yet understanding. They are goal driven and task oriented. Ethics and working within the letter of the law is a cornerstone of their personality. They are readers and writers and are motivated by a sense of fairness and loyalty. Although work values are a priority with the professional, family almost always comes first. Professionals know how to balance their responsibilities. They are organized and management based. Most have a good sense of humor and love life. Some work hard and play hard. Others take huge risks and are rewarded with success and punished in failure; either way, they never give up. Quality of work and life are significant factors in the professional's overall value system. I am proud to report that professionals can be found within the private investigation profession, but you must search for them. If you are aspiring to become a private investigator, this is the type personality suited best for the investigative profession. The problem is there is really not enough income incentive to lure more professionals to the field of private investigation. Misconceptions about the investigative profession created or misrepresented in fiction novels, on television, and in the movies have also had an adverse effect in enticing "the Professional" to the field. Most professionals that usually enter the private investigation profession end up as either agency owners or as command personnel within existing agencies.

Fortunately, most of my employees are "Bus Riders" and "Professionals." And I consider myself lucky. But I'm also a believer in the theory that you make your own luck. You might be wondering how I type myself. What I'll say about that is I consider myself a complex and private person. And since I'm the author of this book, I think I'll exercise my right to remain silent and leave it to you to decide. But instead of trying to figure out my personality type, I suggest you try to determine your own and take corrective action if you find yourself in the less desirable categories.

9
TRIALS & TRIBULATIONS

When I'm getting ready for an argument, I spend one third of my time thinking about what I'm going to say, and two thirds about what my opponent will say.

Abraham Lincoln

Most people who are compelled to go to trial on a civil or criminal matter usually find the process and the event stressful, emotional, laborious, demanding, painful, and costly. It's just not nice. Trials are last resorts for parties that can't manage to get along and settle disputes. Usually, these parties are diametrically opposed in their point of view of the matter in dispute. In the end, the trial turns into a tribulation for at least one party and, if there are multiple parties, maybe more. Criminal and civil litigation is nothing more than a series of motions and hearings to try to get the parties to agree on a settlement, get the case dismissed, or maneuver to a position of strength in the event of a trial. If it doesn't work in the pre-trial phase, a trial takes place to force a settlement one way or the other. In the criminal arena, you are dealing with time, freedom, incarceration, and punishment. In the civil arena, you are dealing with money, injunctive relief (preventing or ordering an action), agreements, and rights. I've thought about this long and hard, and I believe the trial is the tribulation. It usually means negotiation and diplomacy came to an end between people. It means there has been a breakdown in communication between the parties and/or their representatives. Respectful human relations and civility usually cease. Hate can enter the picture. And it means a third party, usually a judge, could not get the warring parties to come together. Judges have chambers for a reason you know. And contrary to mythical belief, they usually don't sleep there. If the parties just can't agree, instead of fighting it out to the death, they go to trial. It's the American way!

But no matter how feeble, the American trial system is the best this world has to offer as a resolution for disputes that can't be worked out. Let an impartial (I sometimes wonder about this) fact finder hear the evidence (they don't always hear all the real facts though) and decide the matter one way or the other. In almost all cases, there will be a winner and there'll be a loser. It has to be that way because the parties force the court to decide issues they were unable to resolve. But in reality, winning in court is sort of an oxymoron the way I see it. What price is to be paid for the win? And who pays?

In a criminal case, there will certainly be a loser. In a sense, however, everyone loses in a criminal trial. Usually, there is a victim whose life has been altered or even ruined. If it's a homicide, the victim is dead and the family and friends are innocent losers; they suffer horrendous heartache. The defendant in a criminal matter is either in jail, about to go to jail, be freed with punishment, or be freed without punishment because he or she was found not guilty or the charges were dismissed. The life of the defendant and the defendant's family has been altered or ruined. The defendant's family and friends are also innocent losers; their heartache is real as well. Even if the defendant is found not guilty, the loss is large. Reputation and character is at stake. Say nothing of the financial toll this takes on both sides. And it's almost always the taxpayer footing the bill because it's the way the system is designed to work and many criminals are indigent; isn't that why they usually commit the crimes in the first place? So we all lose something. Regardless of the outcome, there is no real winner. Yes indeed, there is no doubt in my mind that misery saturates the criminal halls of justice in every courthouse in America five and sometimes six days a week. Thank God there is rest on the seventh day...a respite from the misery...then it starts all over again...and again...and again.

And it's not that much better in the civil arena. Loser... winner....I just don't know. I suppose the party that gets a favorable verdict is the winner and the one that doesn't is the loser. But I guess I just don't see it that way. Money won't heal the wounds or bring back the dead. Money won't repair the scars or comfort the children. Money won't buy you more time or afford you more dignity. Money won't do a lot of things. In fact, it could very well complicate a life to such an extent that whoever it comes to may wish it never came. Those that have to pay, lose money. Those that don't, get to keep it. But the only thing money will do is pay the bills, period! There's always a price to pay. So no matter who gets the verdict, life will be altered. If a plaintiff gets a money verdict, more times than not some insurance company will end up paying the freight, usually with interest, which means the consumer usually ends up paying. If the plaintiff loses (and they are twice as likely to lose as the defendant), at least they would have had their day in court. But we all lose to some extent. It certainly is not the best way to resolve civil disputes. But if people can't come to an agreement or some happy medium, the court system will end it one way or the other. It provides a measure of finality, but not really.

After a criminal or civil trial, the parties are completely spent, emotionally drained, physically tired or ill, and definitely stressed. Some are pissed off. Some are psychologically impaired. Many are in pure agony or superfluous delight. Why people delight in the misery of others is beyond my comprehension, but you see it every day at the local courthouse; perhaps it's because they're just miserable people. It's no wonder court employees seldom look as if they're happy while they're on the job. Ever see a court employee, except maybe a janitor and the court librarian, in the halls of justice after 5 p.m.? I don't blame them for wanting to get out. People loath court because, well, it's a place where human suffering is out in the open for all to see. It's plain nasty! No wonder most people hate to go to court and those that work there love to leave as soon as their day is done.

But it's our way of life. And it has to be that way because those that came before us decided it was best, and we try to improve on it in the present. I don't disagree with them even though I know it's not perfect. Perhaps the biggest problem in a court is there will be times when the fact finder (judge or jury) won't know what in the hell they're doing and a life swings in the balance of incompetence; might as well have that life swing in a noose. The failures are there; they are real; and they are exponentially devastating.

And forget about pure justice. If you're looking for pure justice in a courtroom, look elsewhere. It seldom occurs in any courtroom. You might get a degree of justice, but shouldn't the overall goal be that all parties to an action obtain some measure of justice? I think so. Tell that to the warring parties to the action that firmly believe justice is doled out to clearly favor one side or another. When it doesn't happen for them, they are incredulous and upset. Most of the time, the parties only have themselves to blame. But instead of looking at themselves, most blame their attorneys, the witnesses, the experts, the police, the judge – and they'd blame the court reporter if they could when it doesn't go their way. Oops! I almost forgot? Yes, they blame their private investigator as well. As I said, it's misery.

But justice never completely prevails in the courtroom because it's a winner take all system. It's not "politically correct" and it shouldn't be. To the winner go the spoils! But what about the victims? Both in criminal and civil cases – what happens to them? It's sad, but they are usually forgotten, win or lose. And that's the shame in it. That's the big failure in the system.

Attorneys are obviously an overwhelming factor in the American trial system. But they are *not* the parties. Without the parties, attorneys would have nothing and they sometimes forget that important fact. Attorneys are merely advocates of the parties in dispute. To quote Peter Ettenberg of Worcester, MA, just about the best criminal attorney in the Commonwealth of Massachusetts (and quite possibly the USA): "It's so much worse to be a party than to be an advocate." He's got it right on the money. And some attorneys never get that message. Still, I truly believe most attorneys (including DA's) are good people trying as best they can to work within a system that isn't perfect. For some it's just a job. For others, it's a labor of love. And then for lawyers like Peter, it's a love for the parties and a strong desire to see that justice does prevail and the rights of the people are preserved. With him and other outstanding attorneys, it's not about the money. They are more interested in the evidence than the money. And that's where we come in – the PI, loading the canon with tidbits of evidence so the lawyer can shoot it in court if necessary.

And what about judges, clerk magistrates, court officers, clerks, and staff? No question they are overworked, understaffed, and underpaid. They do the best they can as well, but they usually don't stick around much after 5 p.m., either. They are on the clock and it seems as if they watch it with eagle eyes. How time flies by in life is not analogous to how time moves in the courthouse. Everything moves slowly! Huge case backlogs are the rule and not the exception in many courts (some of which have been created by the unwillingness of defendant's to settle short of trial, and the filing of frivolous lawsuits). It also takes time to make decisions about how matters will proceed (trial or settlement). Preliminary proceedings take time. If it takes a little bit more time to settle a matter, then so be it. Judges do make attempts to have the parties settle the dispute to avoid trial. But it's ultimately out of their hands; the parties make the final decision to settle or not. Time and money are the main motivating factors. Greed creeps into the picture in some cases as you can well imagine.

Once a jury trial is under way, the judge makes the decisions on law and the jury finds the facts. The parties put their full faith in the hands of a judge (even though the jury makes the final decision unless the judge is the fact finder). I have a great admiration and respect for judges. They make numerous decisions about the balance of life each and every day. Some of these decisions are complicated, some simple. The judge sets the rules of his or her court and interprets and applies the law to the case before the court. In all cases, a judge is to maintain order, equity, and fairness to the parties. Judges have a set of rules and guidelines to follow, and most have sweeping authority within their court. But they must follow the law. Sometimes there is trouble, not in following the law, but with interpreting it. The law is subject to interpretation, and that's what judges do, although some do it better than others. If a judge makes an error on the law, the case is subject to be overturned on an appeal to a higher court. Most judges try to avoid mistakes in the interpretation and application of the law. And some judges make lots of mistakes. Thank God for the appeal process. Judicial decisions are subject to judicial review. In jurisdictions where judges are elected, judicial decisions are ultimately judged by the people. I like that. Too bad they're appointed in my state.

Just about the fairest judge that I have experienced is Judge John McCann of Worcester County, Massachusetts. He is a superior court judge (superior court judges rotate from county to county in the Commonwealth). Judge McCann has a contemporary flavor even though he could be my father (I'm forty six as I write this chapter). He is eminently qualified and fair beyond its meaning. Judge McCann is a class act with respect for all parties and lawyers that come before him. What else could you hope to encounter in a judge? He allows jurors to take written notes from opening statements through closing arguments. The jurors before him can ask questions of witnesses. Judge McCann provides jury instructions on the law to the jury *before* the lawyers begin closing statements. And the judge even lets the jurors take a set of the instructions he reads to them in court to the deliberation room. He has a knack for keeping judicial balance in his court. And he's a gentleman. My wife and I had the opportunity to go before Judge McCann on a difficult, personal, and emotional matter as the plaintiff in a wrongful death action. I must say I was impressed with his sense of fairness and ability to apply the law. I have never in my life heard a better set of jury instructions on negligence as applied to a negligence case. And I've heard many over years of investigating negligence cases both for plaintiffs and defendants! You might wonder about the outcome of our case before Judge McCann? To tell you the truth, I don't know yet[9]. The jury is in the middle of deliberations as I write this piece on December 7 (Pearl Harbor Day), 2004. And I'm not changing my opinion of judge McCann, regardless of the outcome. The judge is in Boston at a mandatory meeting and the jury got the day off. I'm pleased that our verdict wasn't decided on a day of significant remembrance. Win or lose (and we're expecting the worst but hoping for the best), I'll always have a tremendous admiration for Judge John McCann. "His honor" is well deserving of much respect and thanks for his sense of fairness, courtroom management style, and respect to the parties, lawyers, jurors, witnesses, and all involved. John McCann is good at what he does, one of the best. No doubt there should be more judges like him. He sets a supreme example. And I happen to know that he's an excellent singer as well.

Other judges I know or have experienced that are good at what they do and are deserving of great respect and admiration are Judge Judd Carhart, who once had the guts to reduce a first degree murder jury verdict to second degree murder (although it should have been reduced to manslaughter in my opinion); Judge C. Brian McDonald, who was the trial judge on the high profile cop killer case Commonwealth v. Eddie Morales that I'll talk about later; Judge Timothy Hillman, a very intelligent and courageous judge who is not afraid to make unpopular, but fair, decisions; Judge Daniel Toomey, a gregarious and approachable man with a great mind whose life was shortened well before his time was done; and Judge George Leary, whose daily decisions affecting the lives of juvenile's in Worcester have great quality of life meaning. Of course, there are many other judges deserving of praise and honor in addition to ones mentioned above that I do not know. Judges have a difficult, but necessary, job to do. And most of them do it very well.

If you have to go before a judge as a party, lawyer, investigator, expert, witness or otherwise, DO NOT dishonor the court or the judge. Treat all people associated with the court with dignity and respect. Do not be impatient because you're not the only item on the agenda. As an investigator, you want to get to know the people who work in the local courthouse, including the judges. Don't be afraid of the judge - they are a lot like you and me and have the same emotions, problems, aches and pains, and frailties as the rest of us. If a judge is familiar with your reputation as an honest, intelligent, caring, and hardworking person, you'll be at ease when that judge has to make decisions that directly affect you. And, who knows, when the judge has to decide on an independent investigator for a matter in court, you just might be the choice.

Every case investigated by a competent professional PI should be investigated and prepared with trial in mind and settlement the goal. Settlement should always be encouraged short of court trial. Remember, a case settled is a case won. Perhaps the most satisfying form of this settlement is in the criminal arena. For instance, a defendant's life is hanging in the balance and you gather the evidence that results in the dismissal of one or more of the charges...like murder or manslaughter. It's happened to me on more than one occasion. In fact, it's happened to me on a number of cases. It's great when that happens, but the attorney may have to force the dismissal. And it's great when the DA agrees to it (which rarely occurs). That's the best outcome of a criminal case because it never gets to trial – it doesn't waste time and loads of money, the misery is much less, and the police and DA can focus on the real issues that plague the community. Justice is served, but never completely prevailed. Why? Because no matter what the outcome, we still have the victim(s). Sure there are circumstances that turn the stomach, such as the defendant that rapes and kills a young female who gets the murder charge dismissed on a technicality. But that's the system – we live and die by it. There are severe injustices on the other side of the coin as well. What about the man who is innocent sitting on death row for thirty years only to be now exonerated by the onset of DNA evidence? Can you imagine doing thirty years in jail for a crime you did not do? How about those people who've lost their lives by execution and were innocent? Wow! Should a government execute their own people when there is even a remote chance that the person being executed is innocent? This is precisely why the death penalty evokes much controversy. It's the system and it's imperfect. As humans, we are imperfect. We make mistakes. So it goes to follow that any system we create will have flaws and foibles.

The professional PI is supposed to help make it better. The professional PI should seek to help the system run smooth and not be a hindrance to it. The hired PI is the face of the attorney client to the lay people involved in the investigation and it's important that the job get done with competence and class.

You are the PI (or if you aren't, pretend you are); the gatherer of fact that the attorney client will try to use to settle the case one way or the other. If the matter goes to trial, you try to help bring some level justice to a system that's flawed but is still the best this world has to offer. The misery will not disappear, but at least you'll be able to go to bed feeling good about yourself, your client, and your client's client. I haven't missed a nights sleep over something I have no control. I've missed a lot of sleep working cases hard so I wouldn't have to miss any sleep over things I do control. Don't you miss any sleep either. The world will be a better place to live and your client should be satisfied.

If you are a professional PI and do your job well, you will make it easier for the American trial system to operate. Make no mistake about it; there will always be warring parties at trial. Bitter disputes will still end up with a winner and a loser. And human suffering will continue in the halls of justice until the dusk of mankind. But that doesn't mean you haven't made an impact. After all, you're on trial every day. You're being judged. Your work is being judged. People will make decisions on your competence after they judge your work; their verdict will mold your reputation and success. Make sure your trials don't become tribulations and you'll almost always come out a winner, no matter which party wins or loses in the courtroom.

10
MONEY MATTERS

I cannot understand why men should be so eager after money. Wealth is simply a superfluity of what we don't need.

Abraham Lincoln

The people who have entered the private investigation business for the money certainly got into the wrong business. What were they thinking? Must have been ill-informed, moonstruck, or just plain nuts! Precious few make the really big bucks. And not many do well financially without some sort of income from another source or a pension from a prior job. So if you're looking to get into the business, do it for any other reason but for the money. Don't misunderstand; you might be able to make millions in the PI business just as in any other. Anything is possible. It's just very unlikely. In fact, you're more likely to find a great white shark lurking in your home swimming pool than to become a millionaire private investigator. I'm certainly not one. And to tell you the truth, I don't know of one. I do know of some PI's and PI retirees who have become millionaires because they invested their money wisely, became involved in other pursuits (even within the profession), or built their business/agency to a point that when they sold out they became millionaires. To become a millionaire by conducting field investigation, chasing deadbeats, locating witnesses, serving process, conducting surveillance, searching out assets, taking statements, and so on and so forth is a tall order. But if striving for that goal is what you want, who am I to tell you to do otherwise. Go for it. The sky's the limit, but you had better strap on a rocket booster if you can find the money to pay for one. Good luck!

I have some news for you: the PI's that are considered the crème of the crop in the profession aren't in the business for the money. They're in it because they love to investigate and help others. If the money comes, it comes. And it does usually come to them because they are the best at what they do. Crème of the crop PI's aren't overly concerned about money as long as they can support themselves, their family, and their pursuits in the profession. They're the ones that can't wait to get up in the morning and go to work - not because they are obsessed with money, but because they love what they're doing. And there aren't many of them.

We all need to get paid for the work we do no matter what it is we do. Some get paid more than others. And it's certainly no different in the PI profession. The *average* field PI gets paid well enough to get by, but not much better. The *average* PI supervisor does well enough to make ends meet and have a little extra. The *average* PI manager pulls in slightly more than the supervisor but is expected to work long hours. The *average* agency owner earns enough to have a little extra dough in the bank and retire with a decent and livable pension, but only if the financial planning is adequate and he or she works their tail off for twenty to thirty years. The point is that few agency owners make millions. On the whole, there just isn't that much money to be made in the PI profession. If you think there is you're fooling yourself. And if some PI tells you there is, they are misinformed. Some industry professionals might say there is plenty of work to go around, and they would be telling the truth. But the law of economics, supply and demand, over pricing, and under pricing keeps the really big bucks from rolling toward the hard working, somewhat successful PI. And though it's true there is plenty of work out there, who gets it? And at what price? You might be surprised at what I'm about to tell you (some will be offended) but I'm trying to communicate a sense of reality. I'm willing to say what has to be said.

PI's are their own worst enemy when it comes to making money. Here's why: *under pricing* and *over pricing.* It's caused mainly by greed, but what else should one expect when money is the motive. It happens in most industries and service based trades, but I notice that it's somewhat prevalent in the PI profession; and we're *supposed* to be professionals. Professional you say! Not when it comes to pricing. Gandhi said: "There is enough in this world for every man's need, but not for every man's greed"[10]. Greed is what hurts PI's more than any other one thing. And jealousy is right behind greed. Eliminate the jealousy and greed and it would be almost utopia in any profession, but especially this one. If I can help eliminate just a smidgen of greed and jealousy in the PI profession by writing about it and hoping someone will listen, I will have accomplished something. And something is always better than nothing...right? Not really. When it comes to money, something is not always better than nothing. If it costs you more money in time and expense to conduct an investigation than what is being paid, nothing is better than something! If you agree to do a full investigation for a flat fee of $1,000.00 and you under priced the job, nothing would have been better than something. You get the point so let's move on.

Under pricing means lowering price just to get work that can't possibly be done for the stated price and little or no profit is realized or a loss is the end result. It's also known as price-cutting, price-gouging, and under-cutting. When someone is under pricing, product quality suffers and the job just doesn't get done right. It can't be done right because the money is just not there to sufficiently fund the investigation. What suffers most, though, is the reputation and credibility of the profession. What's worse is a client oftentimes pays for a poor investigation because some fool PI under priced the job and then couldn't or didn't give the investigation the attention it deserved. The client is now ticked off at the PI and may never hire another one again. The PI then loses the client, makes little or no money, and now has a tarnished reputation. The profession suffers; everyone loses. Motive: greed!

Over pricing is almost as bad as under pricing and it may even be worse. Over pricing means to charge more money for a job and unjustly profit when that same job can be done for less to fairly profit. In other words, price gouging. The motive is – you guessed it – greed! When a PI is over pricing their product or services, it usually means the price is too high for the level of service the PI can supply. For example, an extremely competent PI can charge more money if they have the ability to deliver the product with a greater degree of quality, knowledge, and service than that of a PI with average competence that delivers the product with a lesser degree of quality, knowledge, and service. Therefore, the average PI who charges the same price as the extremely competent PI for the same service in a similar market is over pricing (unless the extremely competent PI is under pricing, but they typically do not under price; otherwise, they wouldn't be extremely competent). The neophyte PI that charges the same hourly rate as the seasoned and experienced PI to conduct the same investigative service in the same or a similar market is over pricing. Over pricing can lead to disappointment, heartache, headaches, screaming clients, failure to pay, disputes, and lawsuits. It also brings discredit upon the profession. We don't want to be known as rip offs or scam artists, do we? Over pricing is done everyday and greed is the motive. To eliminate over and under pricing in any service business, you need to know where you stand to set your price. I touched upon this in other chapters so remember to evaluate your market, the demand for your talents, the true value of your services, and the final product you deliver.

Just how should PI's price their services? It's another million-dollar question, no pun intended. It's tough to put a price on what you think someone is willing to pay you for your time and talents. What will determine fair price is a comprehensive evaluation of the investigation market in your geographical area, your competence and expertise, and a willingness to re-evaluate if market conditions change. If you're starting a business, you need to do your homework and determine what competitors are charging. Once the research is done, you'll have a pretty good idea of what you can and can't charge. Big business will also have something to do with pricing. For instance, insurance companies, large law firms, and big corporations can and do adopt various pricing policies (hourly; flat fee; caps; expense initiative; bonus driven). It's all done to reduce unnecessary expenses and increase productivity. It's what any good businessman should do, so why do agency owners moan and groan when their big business clients want to change vendor-pricing policies? As long as it's fair to the client and the PI agency, there should be no griping, only negotiation. It's an emotional issue, so be cool, diplomatic, and understanding. If you can't profit from a pricing policy, tell the client/potential client why and walk away with a handshake, a thank you, and a smile. Never let them see you sweat. If you can both profit from the negotiated rate and live with it, great. If not, move on. Charging a little less per hour to secure a bulk of business for your agency is good business, but don't under price yourself or the market just to get it; and secure a contract for bulk business if possible. If anyone finds out and questions why you charge "X" company a lower price or hourly wage than you want to charge them, tell them the truth: you have a contract and that "X" company gives you a ton of repeat business. Then you tell the potential client you'd be happy to provide the same level of service for the same price if and only if they will commit to sending your agency a large bulk of business. It can work, but you must be flexible, business savvy, and diplomatic. Don't close any doors or burn any bridges.

I really don't want to get into hourly pricing or flat rates because it's a different market in each area, city, state, country. I would probably agree that if a competent private investigation agency is charging less than $45.00 per hour, then they are under pricing. And based upon what I've seen and heard, I'd have to estimate that the average hourly range of a competent PI agency is between $65.00 and $85.00 per hour. A larger agency with a number of competent, professional PI's may be able to bill up to $125.00 per hour in a large market, maybe not. It all depends on market conditions. Anything above $125.00 per hour I consider price gouging unless the PI is providing specialty expert services or is one of the best the PI world has to offer. There are select agencies in the USA charging upwards of $300.00 to $400.00 per hour, some of whom sub-contract the field investigation to PI's charging well under $100.00 per hour. And you can count these large national agencies using both hands. I've never quite figured out who would pay that kind of money for PI work that is not nearly as good as it should and could be done - for a lot less money! Certainly not worth the kind of bucks some cash cow client is doling out. When the profit margin is six to eight times greater than what these select agencies are paying to have other PI's do the work, it's a sad commentary on corporate PI greed. I would have to guess that their clients just don't know any better. I hope they're reading this chapter.

Now does all this mean that the PI employee working for the agency can make the same kind of money as the agency owner? Absolutely not! Not everyone can be the boss. Nor should everyone be the boss. And if you think you should make as much as the agency owner, think again. The owner takes all the financial risk. The average PI employee doesn't think much about the risk of the agency owner. They see the successful owner driving a new car, sending their kids to private schools, and building a big house. Caveat: Don't let jealousy creep in. Until you *are* the boss, never ever question what the owner charges, earns, or how he spends his or her money because it's really none of any ones business. Make money decisions that directly affect you. Work hard and help lessen the risk of the owner. A good owner will reward you. If not, evaluate your situation based upon facts and not emotion. But be smart. If you have to leave an agency because you believe you're not making enough money, pick up and leave with a handshake, a smile, and good intentions. But watch out; it's not usually greener on the other side of the block, it just may seem that way.

Let's talk about PI employee pay, a subject near and dear to my heart. There is a rule I call "the third rule." *The Third Rule* mandates that a PI agency investigator employee must bill out at least three times his or her hourly or salaried rate of pay in order to be profitable to the agency. So if the agency is billing $75.00 per hour, the most they can afford to pay their top investigator is $25.00 per hour, plus benefits. If an agency pays their top investigator employee a salary of $50,000 per year, that investigator must invoice at least $150,000 per year. Now how is this broken down? It's really simple. One third is the employee rate of pay; one third goes to investigation agency's expenses and the cost of employee benefits; and the last third is agency profit *before* taxes. It doesn't leave a whole lot for agency net profit.

It's tough out there folks. And it doesn't take a brain surgeon to figure out if the agency is invoicing at less that $75.00 per hour then the employee maximum rate of pay must be less than $25.00 per hour. Do the math. You gotta bring in a whole lot of business and have a bunch of employees to do well in the PI world. It's a fact of PI life. Oh well, I hope you're not getting sick on me. I'm already sick just thinking about it.

What about collection of accounts receivables? Oh no! If you aren't sick now, you soon will be. Collecting what is rightfully yours is your right, right? Easier said than done. You want to hope that your clients will pay the bills within fifteen to thirty days; if so, you'll never have a cash flow problem as long as you have the workload. Seldom does it happen in most agencies. I'm lucky because most of my clients pay quick, but not all of them. The key is to do top notch work and the checks will come early. Marginal to poor work quality assures delays; you'll be lucky to get paid.

There are clients who just forget to pay for whatever the reason and need a gentle reminder. Then there are those clients who just don't care when you get paid, or they purposely seek to delay payment. So, if after thirty days you have yet to be paid on an invoice, have your administrative assistant (significant other if you are a one person agency) make a phone call to the lawyer, adjuster, corporate type, private party, or whoever assigned the case and received the report, and communicate a friendly reminder that the invoice is overdue and is expected to be paid as soon as it is received. You want to stay away from it yourself as long as possible so that when you do call the client, they think the unpaid invoice has now become such a problem that it has caught the attention of the agency owner. Resist calling yourself at first because it separates you from the dirty work. I like to be the bearer of good news, not the bad stuff. Nobody likes making these calls, but it must be done. And document each call so there is a record of the call. If you still haven't received payment within forty five days, a letter is appropriate from the administrative assistant. That will usually do the trick unless there is a deeper problem. If the client is the one having the problem, you won't hear from them. If they think your invoice is the problem, you will receive a complaint call almost immediately. If a client has a legitimate complaint, adjust the bill. If not, stand by it. If you are a PI client, take notice; a legitimate complaint *is not* the lack of a desired end result if the investigation was done right.

If a client has ignored paying your bill for a long period of time, call them yourself and inquire as to the problem. Explain the company policy so they hear it from you. Nine out of ten times, the check will be in the mail within a few days. If you haven't received the check within one hundred and twenty days, serious action is required. If it's an insurance company, send the invoice to the adjuster's manager (not the supervisor). Managers hate to be bothered by such matters and the adjuster gets an earful. You'll have the check soon unless there is a deeper problem. If it's an attorney, then complete a small claims action form (usually $5,000.00 and under) and send a copy of the complaint to the firm demanding payment within five days or you'll be left with no choice but to file the suit. You'll get the money pronto. If you don't, then follow through and file the action. And it's the same procedure with corporate and private clients. I have even written the authority that licenses and oversees attorneys. In Massachusetts, it's the BBO-the Board of Bar Overseers. Now that gets the attorney-client's attention. Try to avoid this scenario because you *will* lose the client. The soft but firm touch (an incredible oxymoron) is the best policy because you don't want to lose the client if you can help it. But what choice do you have if the client is not paying your bill? Remember to be professional at all times throughout the process. Take the high road even though you might take a loss. Never send your bill out for collection. Bill collectors harass people, and that's not how you want to be known. If you can't collect it yourself, write it off, learn from the experience, and never do business with the delinquent client again. Or next time, get the money up front.

But you shouldn't have had to deal with these awkward and difficult billing situations in the first place. Retainer and prepayment policies should be established when you form your business and payment policy. In my firm, any case from a new attorney or first time client requires a retainer of at least half the projected cost of the investigation. For domestic and family related investigation, I require the full estimated cost of the investigation up front. And there is *no* exception to the rule. Corporate clients must pay a predetermined retainer. Insurance companies and repeat business from trusted law firms require no prepayment unless the investigation is cost prohibitive. I try to invoice the cases from these clients on a regular basis so there is an interim billing policy in place to support cash flow. Create sound, intelligent business income policies and remain true to them. Never lower your price once you set a flat fee or hourly rate service agreement unless the scope of the investigation has changed. Then you renegotiate. Oh, about retainers; at my firm they are non refundable once the investigation begins. If you adopt such a retainer policy, make sure you let the client know up front.

And what about service contracts? I try to avoid them except for large corporate clients doling out tons of work to my agency. But for attorneys, private clients, small business clients, and the general public, an official contract can muddy up the water. In some states, a contract for services in mandated by law; New York comes to mind for some odd reason. Perhaps it's because they have a shitload of attorneys. Anyway...... When I'm dealing with lawyers, small businesses, and one time corporate clients, what I do to protect myself is *require* a letter from the client assigning the investigation on letterhead along with a retainer; then I send a simple acknowledgement letter outlining the terms. Now you have a contract: an offer, an acceptance, for consideration (money). There's no mumbo-jumbo legalese and people don't get scared off. If the client is someone walking in from the general public or a private party, I get the retainer after full explanation of services so there is complete understanding between the parties. I then write out a receipt for the retainer and balance due (if any) on my letterhead. I write a short paragraph about the service that will be provided by the agency for the fees paid by the client. I sign the letter and have the client acknowledge receipt by signature. Now you have your contract. Sophisticated contracts do not work in simple situations. Don't complicate the situation by creating another headache when you're trying to find a solution to the headache for which the client needs relief. It's just not necessary. Keep it simple.

What about professional courtesies, discounts, or referral fees to referring agencies? How is this handled and do you extend courtesies dealing with money to brother and sister agency owners? Where do I start? Extending professional courtesy is a two way street and is an accepted practice among competent PI agency owners. Most of these relationships between PI agency owners, PI agency employees, and friends of the profession, such as vendors, information providers, and salespersons, are born and further developed at national and state industry conferences and seminars. Once you get to know and trust your brother and sister investigators, the acquaintance can turn into a business relationship and sometimes develops into close friendships. I've been blessed in this regard because my closest friends are other PI's in other PI markets or geographical areas. Don't get me wrong, I have plenty of PI friends in my home state of Massachusetts. Yet I don't refer or subcontract much work inside Massachusetts because it's my state of operation. My primary market is Massachusetts. So it's rare when I need to transact or refer business to a PI friend in Massachusetts mainly because they are direct competitors. But I sometimes refer specialty matters to select Massachusetts PI's if our agency is unable to help a client. I frequently refer business to PI's outside my state when I need an investigation in a specific area other than my direct market. It makes good business sense and it's cost effective. Best of all, it works the other way as well. I receive many referrals from PI's outside of Massachusetts that need investigation within my jurisdiction. Most smart

PI's don't travel to "out of state" locations to conduct an investigation that can easily be referred to a competent PI in that area unless it's a large and sensitive case, the client demands it, or for some other legitimate reason. The traveling PI almost always connects with a licensed PI in the investigation jurisdiction to assist in the investigation. As long as the laws of the jurisdiction are followed, there is nothing wrong with traveling outside your primary market to conduct an investigation, especially if the client requests it and pays for it.

For example, I needed to travel to Ontario, Canada to tell an American citizen living there he had a teenage daughter, but not before I knew what I was walking into. I had just located the subject living with a Canadian woman in Ontario. I certainly did not get any help from the local police. When I called them to ask for assistance it was a nightmare experience. And it wasn't as if I was seeking top-secret stuff or requesting the coordinates of the prime minister's summer cottage. I wanted information on an address, whether or not the owner of the property was familiar to them, and was our subject wanted or known to the local police department. In the United States, ninety nine percent of police officers would provide some level of assistance as long as they understand the request and professionalism is maintained. Here's what I got for a reply from the on duty local police sergeant after I explained what I was looking for: "We don't help PI's." I asked him why. He said, "We just don't do it." The right time of day wasn't negotiable with this jerk. He wouldn't even refer me to a public record custodian or city department that might be able to help me. He would not listen and refused to assist. Why? Isn't it their job to serve and protect? Would he have been serving anyone except himself by his attitude of arrogance?

So I had to hire a PI agency in Ontario and found one in a local urban community of sixty thousand people to initially get me some data. I would have had to hire a local anyway because I would most likely be traveling to Canada as requested by the client. I found a competent PI in Ontario on a referral from a PI association email group. Terry DeGagner helped me out by establishing preliminary information on the subject and the subject's address; he agreed to meet me and Scott Robidoux at 10 p.m. after we drove six hundred fifty miles. Terry accompanied us to the subject's house while Scott and I made the contact and informed the subject he had a kid. And even though Scott is king of the legal pretext, can talk the buffalo off a buffalo-head nickel, and is one of the best physical surveillance investigators in North America, we had our hands full. Can you imagine the many scenarios of this particular situation? Two American PI's are deep into the Canadian bush and we are walking cold onto a Canadian citizen's property to tell her longtime, live-in boyfriend he has a teenage daughter from another woman. Even Terry was a bit nervous about it. The things that could go wrong are simply mind-boggling. Thank God we had Terry, a licensed Canadian PI. If things went down the wrong way and the authorities were called in, we were covered at least from a licensing standpoint.

So we met Terry at a local sports bar and discussed the case and the logistical options. We talked about conducting surveillance and waking the subject up in the early morning but ruled it out. The last thing we needed was a "bush surveillance." We decided it was do or die and that it was best to get it over with. Before we left for the subject's house, we role played the many different scenario's that could occur including what we'd do in the event the subject became hostile and produced a weapon: RUN AND NEVER COME BACK! What if the subject called police? STAY! What if the subject was verbally abusive and loud? NEGOTIATE! What if the subject was cooperative but denied paternity? DIPLOMATICALLY EXPLAIN THE EVIDENCE TO THE CONTRARY! What if he listened but was still recalcitrant and incredulous? ASK FOR A BLOOD TEST! What if he was pleasant, understanding, and admitted he was the father? HAVE A PARTY!

It wasn't exactly a party but the whole event went real well; we had a beer with the subject after the job was done. He admitted paternity after seeing pictures of his daughter and listening to the evidence. He kind of knew anyway but wasn't sure. We made the "wasn't sure" part a definite "sure thing." It was a surreal experience to say the least. The information we obtained on the subject from our investigation and the investigation by Terry DeGagner was instrumental in determining the approach. And Scott Robidoux was fabulous and funny. When we called Terry in from the car about twenty minutes after Scott and I talked our way into the subject's house, he was amazed. Terry couldn't believe his eyes: Scott was taking pictures of me and the subject shaking hands. Next thing you know we're shootin' the breeze with the subject and he's offering us a beer. We were on the road the next day. The client was eventually notified of the success of the meeting and the reaction and response of the subject. If it had been any other way it might have been a nightmare. Success is sweet, but it's sweeter when you team up and do it right.

So you should connect with a local PI when working outside your jurisdiction or the experience could be miserable in more ways than one. It's always better to be legal than to be illegal and certainly better to be safe than sorry.

Now there are unwritten rules to follow when extending professional courtesy (PC), if you elect to participate (I advise you to absolutely extend PC's because what goes around ends up coming around).

Do not offer a referral fee to a referring agency making a client or potential client referral unless the financial capacity of the case is in excess of $10,000. Instead, refer your clients and potential clients who have a case in their jurisdiction to the agency that refers clients to you. Trust is a key issue here. Do this only with reputable PI's with whom you have developed a close relationship.

Never, *ever*, market a referral client without permission from the referral PI agency owner. And do not even broach the subject of marketing the referral client inside the referring agency's jurisdiction. Don't get greedy because word travels fast if you violate this unwritten rule (now written). It's a trust issue. Trust issues loom large.

Discount hourly rates as a professional courtesy if a brother or sister PI assigns a case that you agree to investigate. I reduce my normal hourly rate by at least $10.00 per hour and sometimes more.

When working with other agency owners outside of your jurisdiction and they are the licensee of record, pay them their hourly rate minus an agreeable professional discount.

Always send a retainer check to the PI agency owner conducting a case investigation on your behalf. It's a show of good faith. The agency owner should not have to ask.

Always pay the invoice of an agency owner conducting an investigation on your behalf within thirty days of receipt of such invoice, unless there is a legitimate problem with the work product, authorization, or billing. If a problem exists, try to negotiate a resolution. If you cannot agree, seek a third party to intervene.

Although I shouldn't have to bring this up, I will nonetheless – investigate the referral case as you would any other investigation and keep in mind a PI will be evaluating your product and service. This affects your reputation among other PI's.

I could talk about money until I develop holes in my pockets. It always seems that the more money you have, the more you think you need. Don't let greed get in the way of making sound financial decisions. Greed and jealousy will bring you down real quick so don't over or under value your services or product. You'll never get rich in the PI profession, but you can make a decent and comfortable living if you are fair, reasonable, and diplomatic in business negotiation. Walk away from bad deals with a handshake and a smile. Don't burn any bridges. Remember the Third Rule when pricing and job hunting. Use the soft but firm touch when collecting receivables. Stay away from sophisticated contracts but protect your interest with letter agreements. Extend reasonable professional courtesies to trusted investigative associates and do not violate the unwritten PC rules. And always remember that there are times when nothing is better than something, because money matters.

11

TIME OUT; TIME OFF

My Father taught me to work, but not to love it. I never did like to work, and I don't deny it. I'd rather read, tell stories, crack jokes, talk, laugh- anything but work.

Abraham Lincoln

I don't know many people who love to work. And though I love the work I do, I don't love to work. It's simply not fun to work. If it were, we'd call it "fun" instead of "work." Can you imagine saying to people "I get up at 5 a.m. to go to fun," or "I'll meet you after fun," or "my boss laid into me today at fun?" I rest my case: work is *not* fun. Work is necessary to obtain money in order to live. It's simply a means to an end. But if you are going to work – and most of us have to work – then work hard. And if you are going to work hard, I say play hard. Work hard, play hard. Play hard, but play safe.

In the investigation business, you work long and irregular hours. You're away from your home and family for extended periods. And you'll never earn as much as you'd like, but you can make a decent living; a living that will allow you to take time out of your busy life to take time off. If you work all the time, no matter what you do, you'll experience burnout. Burnout is common in the PI world. That's why time off is very important. And it's important when you do take time off to get as far away from work as possible.

Let's dissect this a bit further. Clients call on investigators to solve a problem or a series of problems. A potential client would not be in my office if he/she did not have some headache that needed a good healing. Most times these headaches and problems are complex (sometimes I get a headache just thinking about it - more like migraines). Now multiply the problems by twenty to thirty times which is the average number of assignments (headaches) in an investigator's caseload which need to be investigated and brought to a conclusion or resolution (usually within two to four weeks). After much time maintaining the caseload, even the most seasoned investigator must get away from it all. And if you hear an investigator say "I haven't had a vacation in years," run away from him fast because he must be nuts or about to go nuts. Probably brain dead. He needs time off!

Most investigators who are competent become brain dead from over use, field abuse, office blues, and running their tail off literally twelve to fifteen hours a day. Now picture an agency owner who conducts field investigation and manages the office and the employees, who are also investigators with twenty to thirty headaches in their briefcase. Not to mention the crap and sometimes unrealistic demands agency owners take from demanding clients. You can only manage this for so long until you either get sick or get sick and tired of it and can't take it anymore. The feeling of pain, insanity of the brain, and melt down madness (not to mention psychosis) one experiences from all this craziness is called *burnout* and you'll need to learn how to deal with it.

I suppose it's great to generate a lot of business and have what some would call "good headaches" – just to set the record straight, there is no such thing as a good headache! But it's certainly no fun (work?) to be running around half crazed, eventually succumbing to burnout.

How do I deal with it? I take a vacation. And if I can't take a vacation, I take a timeout. No, the timeout I'm talking about isn't what parents do to their kids when they've misbehaved. It's more like a timeout in football, except you're not planning your next play. If you're experiencing burn out and a vacation is out of the question, take a day off and stay home and relax. Sleep all day if you must, but don't even think of working. Timeout is a short but sweet time period that will rest the brain from overload. Once rested, the brain will run much better – cognitive reasoning should return to normal and a fresh set of eyes, ears, arms and legs will also run better.

Have you ever heard of a power nap? I'm sure most of you are at least vaguely familiar with the concept. If you believe you can't afford to take a full day off from work, take a power nap time out. It's what I do. And now that I'm getting older (but still younger than fifty), the naps seem to be lasting longer. Nothin' wrong with that my friends...the longer, the better.

I get disgusted when I see self-proclaimed competent investigators go crazy over nothing, get mad about trivialities, talk on the cell phone incessantly during an educational seminar barking orders nonstop to employees about something they can do nothing about; treat their employees with disrespect; are patronizing sycophants; lie constantly; and play one-upmanship. They need to take a nap because they get burned out real fast...mostly from talking too much. About the only thing they're competent at is running their mouths. But the incompetent ones also experience burnout. Let's hope they burnout real fast and get out of the business, but that's not usually the case.

Competent investigators can experience burnout about three to four times a year (unless you're following my recipe of power naps). The experienced ones realize it when it's beginning to set in and take corrective action – power naps, breathing techniques to relax, exercise, walks, and just getting away from work for a short time. The type "A" competents keep going until they nearly kill themselves, then they fly to the Caribbean for a couple of weeks of fun in the sun, sand, and turquoise waters (this was me the first seven to ten years of my PI career). I still vacation in Aruba (I'll probably end up living there someday at least for a few months a year), and I've learned how to enjoy it now. I can call the office when I'm in Aruba (although never more than once a week) and still remain relaxed and focused on my family and my mental health. It sure helps to have wonderful, dedicated employees.

Even some of my good PI friends can't stay on vacation when they're on vacation. They just have to call the office. They can't manage to relax enough where the office can be let go even for a short time. I really don't understand it. This is ok if it works for them, but it's not my style and I don't recommend it to be yours. It creates all kinds of problems with employees as well, both real and imagined; problems dealing with trust, control, communication, and fear.

I won't even mention the family problems that can develop if you work on vacation. Then there can be real headaches (and not the case assignment type) to deal with instead of focusing on real work when you're at work...the kind of work that makes you money.

Bottom line: burnout is a fact of life in the PI world as it is in many other occupations and professions. Take time off when you need it even if you think you can't afford it in time or money. And when you're on vacation, stay on vacation. When you're working, focus on work until your focus is blurred and then stop. Start up again when you are refreshed. You'll be able to go many, many productive hours if you take care of yourself.

And remember...without health, no matter what else you have, you have nothing.

12
STUDY HALL

Get the books, and read and study them till you understand them in all their principal features; and that is the main thing. It is of no consequence to be in a large town while you are reading. The books, and your capacity for understanding them, are just the same in all places.

Abraham Lincoln

Resource period. In my day it was called "study hall." Oh how people love to change the name of things that supposedly portray a negative image – you know, the spitballs across the room slamming into female cleavage. Few would argue that "study hall" conjures up horrific and repressive thoughts in the minds of yuppie crazed high school administrators. It led to the name change. The classic name change example is when the manufacturer changed the name of my favorite cereal from Sugar Pops to Corn Pops[11]. Cripes, it is what it is. But I'm almost positive it was a matter of money, too. Don't most things boil down to money? I think so. I know so! I think the cereal caper happened about the same time "study hall" became "resource period." Probably not the same person making the decision, but certainly the same lame brain mentality.

I'd sure like to know what students do in "resource period" in America's high schools today. They're probably all eating Corn Pops. I'll bet it hasn't changed too much from the old days, except for the name. The "meet the new boss, same as the old boss,"[12] syndrome is alive and well. It's still good to know that the more things change, the more they remain the same; except for the feel good names. I guess the people making the decisions on these matters are smarter than me so I'll just leave it in their capable hands.

All kidding aside (and I'm not kidding), study hall had two tremendously redeeming values. First, you had the opportunity to get your study or homework done. Second, you socialized (if, and only if, you didn't have killjoy teachers and you kept your voice level below that of a screaming banshee). I don't know about you, but I looked forward to study hall. And it's no different for me today than it was thirty or so years ago. I'll explain a little later. But for now, let's get into training, continuing education, and professional development in the PI world. That's where the study hall comes in, minus the spitballs of course. You'll see.

The standard form of training and continuing education for most people is school –elementary school, then Jr. and Sr. high school, then college, and possibly a post graduate program leading to a master's degree and maybe even a doctorate. In my opinion, there is no tried and true schooling or training program for professional private investigation. In a perfect world, it would be wonderful if there were a viable, accredited school that could grant a state license to be a professional private investigator upon completion of their training. Guess what? It's not a perfect world and, as of this writing, there is no such school. It just doesn't work that way. Governments control licensing; schools do not. Nevertheless, there are a few schools that do have a viable certificate or associate's degree program, or are in the development stages of creating a program, in professional private investigation. But not one of them can put you in business or guaranty you a job. It's the same in *any* high school or college degree program as well. Just as in life, there are no guaranties or promises that can be made when you set out to start your new beginning.

But at least there are job placement offices at most colleges and some high schools, right? A lot of good that'll do you. I can't answer for others, but I have never once received a phone call from a high school or college job placement office asking if there was a job opening or inquiring to place a candidate into a private investigation job that I had advertised was available. I have even called placement offices and requested referrals of students or graduates possessing a specific skill set that would match well at my PI agency. It has never once worked out for me or my company. And I'm a big supporter of education and school-sponsored programs. My wife and I graduated from public high schools and colleges. We now send our two oldest children to private high schools and my son is about to enter a well known college. My youngest child is in a public elementary school at present, but will attend a private high school. Our commitment to education and training is steadfast and true. And it has extended to the private investigation profession as well.

So what is the problem with the transition from school to job? It seems to me, and it's just an observation, that there's a little too much theory and book teaching and not enough practical hands on experience going on at most traditional schools today. Educators are relying on corporate America to train new hires *how* to work once they become college educated and are recruited. It's one less thing they have to do and doesn't drain the budget. Some schools are addressing this problem head on and new "hands on" programs are being developed that certainly help, but it's a long way from perfection. In the private investigation business, most agencies are small companies with one or two employees. Agency owners do not have the time or money, nor are they likely to have developed a written program or manual, to train new employees. And unless the potential new hire with little or no experience wants to work for next to nothing, training to become a PI usually isn't going to happen at the average PI agency. Doesn't sound right, does it?

The bottom line is profit; most agencies cannot afford to train and develop a new employee. They leave it to the larger agencies (which are few and far between), insurance companies, government, and related big business to train and develop new hires so they can hire experienced investigators away from them when they need them. I rely upon this system to some degree, although we do train new hires as well. A newly hired, experienced investigator can become immediately profitable after a short adjustment period with the small agency. A tenderfoot right out of college or graduation from a private investigation training program can be a financial liability for months. Unfortunately, small agencies cannot wait it out in most cases. Some agencies hire interns from colleges that grant credit for the work experience, but that requires training. Training cost money. And not many agency owners are willing to train someone who they'll probably never see again after the internship has ended. But some do.

And what's the deal with formal colleges for private investigators? Degree programs in criminal justice are abundant and most are targeted for law enforcement or those wanting a career within some area of police sciences. Law enforcement deals with the safety of citizens and the investigation of criminal matters from a prosecutorial vantage. There are limited civil, corporate, and private sector applications taught within a criminal justice program. And since I've already indicated there are only a few accredited degree programs in the field of private investigation offered by colleges, criminal justice is sometimes a forced choice for those choosing a career in an occupation related to investigation other than law enforcement. But I need to tell you, I'd rather interview a potential candidate for a position in my investigation agency that has a BA degree in liberal arts with a concentration in any one of the following areas: English, history, political science, sociology, philosophy, criminal justice, and the acting arts. Why? I have found that most people with BA degrees are hands down better writers, speakers, managers, and communicators than those with a BS degree. And the secondary reason is this: it's simply my choice. I offer my apologies if you are insulted; it's just my normal policy. From time to time, there will be the potential employee with a BS in Criminal Justice that is a strong candidate for a career as a PI (and I have hired them). But I prefer those with a BA degree. Perhaps you might wonder if it has something to do with the fact that I have a BA degree in the liberal arts; I doubt it. I base my decisions on past experience and thinking through situations that are before me. I make judgments based upon fact, not bias or prejudice. The better writer and speaker win every time, hands down, at least in private sector investigation when someone like me is making the evaluation. So sharpen up those pencils, or should I now say keyboards?

Let's get back to the study hall and private investigators. Training, continuing education, and professional development in the PI profession are almost always sponsored by state, national, or international associations, or a combination thereof. For this reason alone, membership within state and national PI associations is a must. Some states statutorily mandate continuing education credits (CEC's) for renewal of the PI license; it's contained within their licensing requirements. This is a good thing, although can you imagine that some PI's believe otherwise. CEC's should be mandatory in each and every state now that there are a plethora of educational conferences and seminars that provide excellent education and training. Almost all credible association sponsored certification programs in the investigation profession require CEC's to maintain the certification. Most mandatory CEC's for those investigators who are certified in one specialty or another (they must maintain the education to keep the certification current) are obtained at professional conferences and seminars.

The key words are "conferences and seminars." Conferences and seminars deliver training and education to the PI. Conferences and seminars unite PI professionals that share and discuss common business goals. Conferences and seminars help maintain and expand business and social relationships with other PI's, vendor representatives, guests, expert speakers and instructors, and friends. Professional investigation conferences and seminars bring credibility to a profession that has been maligned for many years. Conferences and seminars allow PI's to come together in peace to ensure that access to public records and other tools essential to do the job is not legislated away. And since most PI conferences and seminars are open to the public, these educational and social forums introduce the profession to those who are interested in private investigation as an occupation.

There is intense competition among associations to sponsor and market training and educational conferences because they can be big money makers, especially in states that mandate CEC's and among associations that sponsor certification programs. So it goes to follow that there are quite a few conferences and seminars in the USA and across the oceans to consider attending. Some are superb. Some are good. Some are not so good. And some are just plain terrible. When the motive is money first and everything else second to money, watch out.

In much the same way they can be big money gainers, conferences and seminars can also be money losers in a big time way. There are some long standing, viable investigation associations that have been to the ringer and back with conferences that have gone bust. Why? Inexperience and indifference of the organizer is the major cause; lack of attention; outdated or nonexistent procedural policies; failure to effectively negotiate with providers, especially hotels; and general apathy within the profession and among association membership. I can talk forever on just how pathetic the apathy rate is within the profession regarding attendance at professional PI conferences and seminars. It begs for fixing and that is one of many reasons why I'm a big fan of mandatory CEC's. I'd estimate (and it's a liberal estimate) that about ten to twenty percent of those employed *and* active as full-time private investigators regularly attend professional development and continuing education conferences and seminars. This means eighty to ninety percent DO NOT regularly attend a training seminar; that is shameful! And then again, maybe it isn't (you might have to think about this for a few seconds before it dawns on you especially if you're one of the ones who don't attend). Wow! What a sad commentary. Let's extrapolate further. If there's forty thousand active PI's in the USA, and you accept my liberal percentages, then there are between thirty thousand and thirty six thousand PI's who are not receiving regular continuing education and training to stay sharp, knowledgeable, and up to date with changing methods, technology, different theories of investigation, advances within the profession and related fields, and new and proposed legislation. No wonder it's tough to find a good, competent PI. Conferences and seminars are a must!

Major considerations regarding a decision on which conferences to attend are many. Who is coordinating and running the show? Is there a team or committee helping the coordinator? What is his or her track record? The venue – will it be located in an area that is fun and easily accessible? Cost is also a factor. When you or your firm is shelling out megabucks to travel to and attend a conference, you want value. You want state of the art and hands-on seminars and educational instruction. You want to see world-renowned experts as instructors. You want an entertaining speaker at the major social event. You *do not* want to be bored. So the educational *and* social program is important, but so is the trade show aspect of the conference. The "trade show aspect" of a conference means will there be investigative vendors, service providers, and sales representatives to display and show their services and products to attendees for potential purchase. So make sure there are a good number of diverse vendors and exhibitors. The "social aspect" of a conference is also a significant factor. Some have no social events; others have a lot, but most have a good mix. I like the ones with a good mix of education, training, tradeshow, and social events. Social events are important because people get to know each other, share information, become friends, and refer business to each other. And if you're new in the field or contemplating private investigation as a professional career, what better way to see and be seen, hear and be heard, and get to know and get known?

Although the old adage of "bigger is not necessarily better" may apply to most things, such has not been the case with investigative conferences. The birth of the "Super Conference" has revolutionized the investigative profession in the area of professional development and continuing education. Very few people can effectively run a PI Super Conference in the USA; you can count them on one hand. Super Conferences are all inclusive to professional investigators and their spouses, family, and friends. They are sponsored by a variety of state, national, and international associations. Uniting the profession is a main theme of the Super Conference. There may be fifteen to twenty association sponsors and forty plus vendors/exhibitors. Some exhibitors are sponsors as well. There are usually twenty to thirty instructors and speakers in multi tracked investigative disciplines. Now this may not seem big by comparison with seminars and conferences sponsored by other groups representing teachers, police, doctors, and lawyers. But there's a lot more of these professionals in the world than PI's- that's for sure. Everything is relative.

The New Orleans Super Conference coordinated by Julius "Buddy" Bombet and the Northeast Super Conference (NESC), hosted by yours truly, have extended the boundaries and set the supreme standard of professional development and continuing education within the PI profession. Few would dispute it. Buddy Bombet is a close personal friend and a contemporary mentor. He is considered the "Father of the Super Conference." Buddy penned the name "Super Conference." The first one was held in New Orleans in 1997 and was a smashing success. I took the idea to the northeast and put a northern flavor to it. I try to run one of these Super Conferences every other year, but it's tough. I've run three of them since 1999 and I'm about due for another. The last NESC was held at the Borgata Hotel and Casino in Atlantic City, NJ. It was the largest Super Conference ever held in the PI world and still holds that distinction as of this writing. Marcia Clark of O.J. Simpson case fame was the keynote speaker and was a pleasant surprise to some doubters. I had dedicated committee members working their tails off and they really deserve the credit, not me[13]. And the staff at my PI agency was great[14]. You can't possibly do these Super Conferences alone. It takes a great deal of time and energy to administrate and coordinate these beasts, but it's well worth it. I take no money for myself. I volunteer my time and service to a profession that has given much to me. It's the least I can do. I like to give because I have been given to. It feels good to pass the generosity on when you are able. I recommend generous and charitable service no matter what occupation you choose. Remember, what goes around usually ends up coming around. Give back what you take, and then give back a little more. You'll set the example for the next generation.

There are many other excellent regional conferences and seminars that are co-sponsored by more than one PI association and are not considered Super Conferences. And then there are the superb "stand alone" conferences sponsored by one association, be they an international, national, or state association. Credit must be given to the hard working people who run these events as well. It takes a Herculean effort to run any good-sized conference or seminar, and I am truly appreciative to those professionals that run a tight and true ship to assure the overall success of the event. It makes all PI's look good. It brings character, integrity, and dignity to the profession. It promotes professionalism. It educates the PI willing to be further educated. But what's most important is it benefits the clients and enriches their lives and the lives of those that surround them.

Now what is it about the study hall (or resource period) that I look forward to when I attend these events? It's a break from the action when I'm not running the show. It's just as in the old high school days. Nothing has really changed except the names and faces of those you study with and, of course, your age. You study a little and socialize a lot. Then you study a bit longer and socialize a little more, and so on until the next one rolls around. You make friends, just as you did in high school and college, and some of these friends become your best friends. You meet up at these study halls that can take place in just about any place in the USA or, as a matter of fact, the world. About the only difference is there are no bells and nobody forces you to attend class. I don't have to be forced because I now understand the true value of the study hall. And I'm still eating Sugar Pops...oops, aghh, excuse me, *Corn Pops* as well.

13
AGAINST ALL ODDS

I claim not to have controlled events, but confess plainly that events have controlled me.

Abraham Lincoln

Sisyphus! Ever hear of him? Unless you've studied Greek Mythology, he was probably not on your top ten list of celebrities...and even still. And no, Sisyphus was not a sissy; quite to the contrary. Sisyphus is said to have been the founder of Corinth, later to become the Corinthian King at the hands of Medea. Sisyphus had a tough life. His children with Tyro were killed by Tyro herself because they were supposedly destined to kill Tyro's father, Salmoneus, who was also Sisyphus's brother. It makes little sense to me, but who am I to question the storyteller. After all, it's only a myth. Sisyphus is best known in mythology because he ratted out Zeus to Asopus (Zeus is said to have stolen off with Asopus's daughter). Because he failed to keep his mouth shut, Sisyphus is condemned to the *Underworld* forever; his punishment is to roll a huge stone with his hands and head up a slope to the summit of a hill. Seems easy enough. But the perennial problem is the stone always rolls back to the bottom of the hill when the job is nearly finished. The stone will never set on the summit. Sisyphus toils ceaselessly to accomplish the task time and time again. The goal cannot be reached. No matter how hard he tries, the effort is never ending. The torment and torture lives on forever. He becomes exasperated but never quits. Such a task mandated by the Gods was, as designed, *against all odds!* It wasn't going to happen. And for all we know, he is still rolling that stone. Someday, maybe the stone will come to a final rest at the top of the hill. I hope so for Sisyphus's sake. In any event, the myth leaves one to wonder: Why would anyone continue to work in vain when the goal can't possibly be achieved? The Gods don't answer this important query. They leave it for us to decide.

And so it will be with any person who is facing a similar situation. There will be times when your work will feel like a punishment. There will be times when you will question the purpose of the work. There will certainly be times when you feel the end result of the work is meaningless. You'll question whether the means justifies the end; and more importantly, whether the end justified the means. You may become agitated and lose hope; and that's the last thing you want. Don't dare to give up on hope. To do so is to admit defeat before the work is finished. And it may never finish the way you'd like it to end. So you press on and you wonder why. The answer may never come, but you do what you have to do because it's what you're supposed to do. It's what you're used to doing. And sometimes this work is a fruitless but necessary labor. Or at least it seems that way.

A professional private investigator never gives up on hope, even if the task seems insurmountable. There are times when I have felt just as Sisyphus did when working cases that seemed beyond my reach, or for that matter, beyond the reach of anyone. I have a name for doing work where the goal is clearly out of reach; I call it the "*Sisyphus Syndrome*." Here's how it usually goes. I roll the stone to the top of the hill to its final resting spot. And just as I'm about to roll it into place, the stone falls backward and rolls all the way back down the hill over the same path in which it came. I stand there watching it roll back. I think about all the hard work I expended, all for naught. I become frustrated and angry. Frustration and anger soon turns to determination. Determination then turns to recalcitrance. I will not let this happen no matter what. I shall not accept this fate. Someone is depending on me. I decide to try again. I walk back down the hill with a sense of purpose. I start all over again; and if need be, again and again. It's how tough cases are solved. It's how due process is maintained. It's how the system survives. It's how hope stays alive. It's how miracles happen.

But I am not a miracle worker. I leave the miracles to a higher power. I'm interested in helping my clients. I'm interested in helping others. And I'm interested in doing the absolute best I can do. If a miracle happens along the way, then great; if not, then that's okay too. And just because I don't depend on miracles doesn't mean I don't pray for them to happen because I do. There are times when the client cannot be helped and praying may be the only measure of personal resolution left. But I refuse to feel hopeless when the inevitable is clearly out of my hands. I must depend on faith. So do what you must, but do something.

Every so often there'll be a client that comes along with a problem so substantial that the odds of helping this client are in the millions, or even billions, to one. Then there'll be cases you take on that seem fairly routine, only to turn into a fight with a fire-breathing dragon. And there are investigations that seem exceedingly difficult at first and turn out to be relatively easy to work and solve. Then there are the rest that fall in the middle. It's the nature of the business. A top professional private investigator will recognize the degree of difficulty of a potential investigation during the client consultation, even the ones that seem routine but are nightmares waiting to be dreamt. The case investigation will be priced based upon the degree of difficulty, not exclusive to hourly rate but by the time, expense, and level of expertise of the investigator. The actual hourly service rate will usually remain the same throughout the investigation. There will and should be large retainer requests for investigation cases that are determined to be extremely difficult, time consuming, and/or labor intensive. In just about all cases, the clients know when their particular case is beyond difficult. Some will try to downplay the degree of difficulty, but they probably know the score so it doesn't take much to educate them if they don't quite (or pretend not to) understand the complexities. If the investigation cannot be adequately financed or the client is unwilling to pay the price, I decline to work the case no matter how challenging or provocative it may seem. Without proper financing, no investigator can get the job done and be even close to successful. And isn't it the same in all occupations and professions? You certainly get what you pay for and you can take that to the bank (no pun intended).

I've turned down some huge, complex, and high profile cases. I've taken on the challenge of criminal defense cases in which the complexities of investigating and solving the crime was not even an issue; at issue was theory of defense and due process. When a client has been convicted of first degree murder and sentenced to death, what becomes complex is trying to save a life that in all likelihood cannot be saved (do not condemn me if you support the death penalty because I am not debating whether or not a life should or should not be taken by laws that allow it). When the client is guilty of committing a crime and you are hired to investigate for the defense, the complexity is in the theory of defense, assuring due process, and establishing the investigative theme; then and only then can you execute the investigation. When you are hired to investigate a forty year old missing person case that even the federal government cannot solve, the complexity is in unraveling the mystery and not in establishing an investigative plan (although the plan is important). When hired by a victim's family to re-investigate an auto fatality or catastrophic injury in which the police and/or the insurance company have investigated and made an adverse determination on causation (the victim was at fault), the challenge is in establishing the facts over and beyond any failures of those who have previously investigated the incident, or eventually convincing the client that the investigators did their job and the victim made an error in judgment if the evidence leads to such a conclusion. It's tough out there, folks. These cases are not easy. Life and death decisions are made based upon the outcome of investigations of this nature. It is much too easy to turn these arduous and complex matters down and leave them to another. But these are the ones that keep you sharp. They are the ones that encumber the mind and touch the soul. They are the ones that keep you up at night and inhibit your thoughts during the day. They consume you. And you consume them. They are the cases that are almost impossible to win and are what I consider investigation *against all odds.* They are "David and Goliath"[15] cases. They challenge the mind, tax the body, and invigorate the spirit. I truly love doing them. Many PI's are afraid of them; and that's one of the many reasons why I agree to take these cases. Someone must do them, so it might as well be me. It could be you. And if it has been you, you know what I'm talking about.

I've done so many of these cases I could literally start writing about them and never stop. I want to discuss two such cases (both murder cases) in which the Sisyphus Syndrome was an obvious factor from onset to completion; one I did from pre-trial through trial, the other one (a death penalty case) was done post-conviction by my good friend, Colorado criminal defense investigator, H. Ellis Armistead[16]. It's tough for any PI who works murder cases to talk about them for a number of reasons but confidentiality issues still in place long after disposition of the case are the number one reason. Another significant factor lies in the emotional and psychological impact the case has on the lead defense investigator. And third, talking about death is just plain depressing. But here I go anyway[17].

Commonwealth of Massachusetts verses Eddie Morales[18]

John DiNapoli was a good cop, but a better man. He was a hero to most who knew him; an icon. His life was dedicated to helping others. That is until it was cut short by bullets one cold, gray December morning in Holyoke, Massachusetts. It was 1999 and just three days before Christmas. The community was shocked. The manhunt was on. And, boy, was it a manhunt. A twenty-one year veteran cop had been gunned down while on the way to run an errand. Officer DiNapoli didn't know what hit him just before his life ended. He didn't have to die. At least not like this. Ten bullets riddled his white unmarked Crown Vic. Five bullets hit the officer; one shattered his aorta. He never had a chance.

And neither did Eddie Morales. He knew what he did. And as he had done throughout his life to avoid responsibility, he ran. He didn't know any better. Eddie Morales had been running since he was a child. The twenty seven year old from Arroyo, Puerto Rico was a product of the environment in which he knew and grew; one that was void of direction, love, proper parenting, and discipline; one that was full of neglect, anger, desperation, and crime; and one that involved drugs and guns. But guns don't kill people; people kill people...Why? I'll bet the family of John DiNapoli asks *why* each and every day. I know I do. I can't stop asking why! Perhaps it's because I keep searching for an answer that can't be found.

It was about 9:00 a.m. on December 22, 1999 when Police Officer John DiNapoli responded to a disturbance call at the intersection of Sargeant and Walnut Streets in Holyoke, MA. DiNapoli was on his way back to the police station after dropping another officer off at Juvenile Court when he decided to take the call. Because he was assigned to administrative duty at the Holyoke Police Station, DiNapoli was in plain clothes, unarmed, and without vested protection. Although his unmarked vehicle had police lights above the rear view mirror and a siren, DiNapoli never activated them; no one knows why. After chasing Morales with the unmarked white car about three hundred fifty yards through an alley and into an intersection, Eddie Morales emptied a 9mm semi automatic handgun through the front windshield of the car fatally wounding John DiNapoli. And then he ran.

Morales fled Holyoke in short order after ridding himself of the weapon. There was an intense dragnet in Holyoke and the surrounding area, and a nationwide alert and manhunt. The slaying made national news. Thousands of law enforcement officers were on the lookout for Eddie Morales. Hundreds were attempting to track him down. There was never any other suspect. This crime was committed in broad daylight in a multi-ethnic, poverty-stricken, drug-infested neighborhood. It was 9:00 a.m. People were all around the direct vicinity of the scene. There were fifteen eyewitnesses to the shooting and it's aftermath that came forward, and I'm sure there were a lot more that we'll never know about. Sixty-three witness statements were taken by police within a matter of days. Eddie Morales was identified as the shooter many times over. The 9mm Norinco Model 213 black semi automatic handgun found and identified by a witness as the gun Morales used (found in a white trash bag and set out on Hampshire Street as trash) was matched to ballistics evidence recovered from the scene, from the bullet pierced unmarked vehicle, and from the body of Officer DiNapoli.

Morales was tracked and subsequently apprehended in Scranton, Pennsylvania on December 27, 1999. Morales waived extradition, cooperated with local and state police, and was brought back to Holyoke in the handcuffs that belonged to the slain officer while the world watched with great delight.

During the interrogation in Scranton, Eddie waived his Miranda rights (you know, the "you have the right to remain silent" ones,) and gave two voluntary statements: one to Scranton Police and the other to the Massachusetts State Police (MSP). MSP sent Lt. Peter Higgins and Troopers Daniel Soto and John Murphy to Pennsylvania to recover the suspect. They were the three lead police investigators on this case and conducted a thorough and competent investigation. By all accounts, the statements Eddie Morales gave to police were unmitigated confessions.

Here's what he told police (and keep in mind that English is not Eddie's first language):

In his two police statements, Morales admitted to police that he was selling drugs on a street corner on the morning of December 22, 1999 and eventually got into a fight with a Hispanic guy in a blue car who was trying to rob him. He punched this Hispanic guy in the face and then the guy left, saying, "I'll be back." Eddie told police he retrieved a black automatic gun hidden in an alley because he thought the Hispanic guy was coming back to get him. He started to return to the street corner when a white car pulled up and the driver pointed at Eddie and said "stop right there." Eddie started to run and ran down an alley. He told police he tried to get rid of his drugs and the gun he had on him in the alley. The guy in the car was coming after Eddie so he ran left onto the street. The car was about twenty feet away when Eddie ran to the sidewalk. Eddie told police "I got so nervous that I started shooting at the front window of the white car. I was stopped right there and shooting. I don't know how many times I shot." He said he dropped the gun and ran. Eddie told police he got a ride to the Greyhound bus station by an unidentified black male. He stated he then took a bus to Philadelphia. Eddie told the police he was unable to find an un-named friend in Philadelphia so he took another bus to Scranton, PA where he remained until his apprehension. He met up with and stayed with a boyhood friend in Scranton.

Eddie's boyhood friend from Arroyo, Puerto Rico, and his girlfriend, then living in Scranton, called Holyoke police when they learned what Eddie had done (I'm sure the $50,000 reward money also had a little something to do with it). They were then contacted by Scranton Police and the details were planned for the arrest. They delivered Eddie Morales to Scranton Police in a shopping plaza parking lot where the arrest was made without incident. But I have to question the wisdom of arresting Morales in a shopping plaza in broad daylight with many people around. Can you imagine the fallout had there been a shootout and an innocent bystander was hurt or killed? Whatever made the Scranton Police think Eddie Morales wouldn't fight to avoid arrest after shooting a police officer down five days earlier? Especially when the officer was trying to apprehend him! I wonder about this a lot, for more reasons than one. Oh well...thank God it went down without a hitch.

After he was brought back to Holyoke and appeared in court for arraignment, Jobeth DiNapoli, Officer DiNapoli's distraught but classy twenty five year old daughter, said "I've never really felt any anger toward this man. I feel bad for this man. He obviously never had a John DiNapoli in his life."[19] She was absolutely right.

Peter L. Ettenberg of Worcester, MA was the private attorney hand picked by the Committee for Public Counsel Services in Boston to represent the indigent Eddie Morales, who was arraigned on December 29, 1999. Ettenberg was selected because the Commonwealth wanted to be sure no legal errors would be made in which to base an appeal of a likely conviction. They knew Morales would be getting the finest defense possible with Peter Ettenberg – he's that good. In fact, he's *the best.* And Peter had prior experience with a cop killer as he represented one of the defendants who were charged with murder in the shooting death of Paxton, MA Police Chief Robert Mortell in 1994. Peter had no reservation about taking the case, although he confessed privately that he had no idea where he was going with the defense. Peter looked at it as strictly business but his client was Eddie Morales, and this client was the guiltiest scum on the face of the Earth to almost all people in the Commonwealth of Massachusetts and beyond. Peter was feeling the heat, but he never let it affect him. In a December 1999 interview with Gary Murray, long time Legal Reporter for the Worcester Telegram & Gazette, Ettenberg said "Unless and until there's a conviction, my client is not guilty."[20] In reality, Peter new that the presumption of innocence was little consolation in this case given the mountain of evidence against Eddie Morales. And so did I.

I was hired by Ettenberg to head up the defense investigation and put together the defense investigation team, but not until May of 2000. It was a depressing New Year for a lot of people, including Peter Ettenberg. For me, I knew it was coming. Even though I had to wait, investigating a no win police killing case wasn't quite what I had planned to ring in the new millennium. Six months had passed since the slaying and Peter sent me an overview of the case with a letter saying, "Let me know what you want to do." After reading the overview, I called Peter and told him there wasn't much we could do except look (more like peek) at self-defense. He said, "Find me self defense!" I said "Okay, pulling rabbits out of hats is now my specialty." Over the next ten months, Peter and I would cement our business and personal relationship.

It took me more than a month to get all discovery documentation (statements, reports, photographs, evidence sheets, logs, Grand Jury minutes, video, notes, and all sorts of related paperwork). It was enough to fill a filing cabinet. I then went to work finding a defense in self-defense.

Simply stated, the self-defense defense in Massachusetts involves satisfying three legal elements:

1) The defendant must reasonably be in fear of serious bodily injury or death.

2) The defendant must have no real chance of escape.

3) The force used by the defendant must be reasonable and necessary

I put together a defense investigation team that included crime scene and blood spattering expert, Stuart James from Ft. Lauderdale, Florida; former MSP Lieutenant and expert ballistician Billy Duke of Cape Cod; Spanish speaking investigator Rob Diaz from Worcester, MA (Diaz accompanied me on every trip to Holyoke when it involved tracking and interviewing witnesses); and Tricia Bonzey from my office, who did all the administrative work and a good bulk of office investigation in support of the field investigation. I reviewed all discovery materials received ten times over and then some. Trish indexed the discovery (there were many indexes) to keep me organized, focused, and to help me properly handle and manage the investigation. I found the theory of defense of self-defense in six eyewitness statements and the two statements of Eddie Morales taken by MSP. The complexity of the case really came down to the simplicity of passages from the eight police statements. The tough part would be convincing a jury that the force used by Eddie Morales to ward off a white car that was barreling down on him was reasonable. It would eventually prove to be impossible. As I said, the Sisyphus Syndrome was pervasive. Even still, hope was never abandoned.

It was now time to interview Eddie Morales. On July 31, 2000, I went to the Worcester County House of Correction in West Boylston, MA (about four miles from my office) and met Eddie Morales. He was not the monster I had expected by any stretch of the imagination. Eddie was calm, polite, respectful, and remorseful. He was also thankful that Peter and I were helping him. With tears in his eyes, Eddie said "I want you to know how thankful I am to you...nobody has ever helped me like this in my life." I was amazed and surprised. I told him I could only help him if he told me the truth. And I never passed final judgment on Eddie Morales until the jury verdict. I spent many hours with Eddie over the next few months. I treated him with dignity and respect and maintained professionalism. I gained his trust. He never ever let me leave him without saying thank you. I began to feel bad for him – nobody ever really cared about him, not even his parents. His mother and father never once stepped foot inside the court room to support him or at least showed they cared. Everyone deserves someone to care about them and love them, no matter what. Even Eddie Morales! As I said, Jobeth DiNapoli was right on the money with her speculative perception and comment of Morales. Eddie "never had a John DiNapoli in his life."

Eddie told me everything. He admitted he lied to police about some of the things he told them but only to protect the friends who helped him after the shooting. Eddie never told his friends what he had done because he did not want people implicated in a shooting they had nothing to do with. He didn't even want to tell me the real story but finally ended up giving me *all* the information. Eddie told me he first learned the victim was a cop when he spoke to his girlfriend two hours after the shooting. And for you doubters out there, you can believe what you want to believe. Eddie Morales did admit he pulled the trigger. He admitted to the killing. I even detected remorse in Eddie Morales as he made the admission. He had always maintained he did not know the driver of the white car was a cop. He claims to have been defending himself. It was a claim few people would believe, especially since he refused to testify. He wouldn't testify because he didn't want to give up his friends (most of these so-called friends turned on him in a heartbeat). Eddie also realized that if he *was* to testify he'd have to call the cops liars and wondered who would believe him. I wondered as well. So did Peter Ettenberg.

A rather important factual issue that was hotly disputed by the defense *and* the prosecution was whether or not Eddie Morales knew the operator of the white car was a police officer. There is no question that in his first statement to Scranton Police, Eddie clearly states *"I'm sorry for what happened; I didn't know he was a cop."* In the second statement given to MSP at the Scranton Police Station later the same day, Eddie stated, *"I thought it was a cop, so I started running."* Eddie maintains he never told MSP he knew or thought the driver of the white car was a police officer. Morales told me that MSP Lt. Higgins was pressuring him during the statement taking process in Scranton and quoted Higgins saying many times over "of course you knew it was a cop." We'll never know the real truth because there was no third party in the interview room-only MSP Investigators and Morales know for sure. But I often wondered (and still do) why a Scranton police detective wasn't in the interview room with MSP during their interrogation of Morales at the Scranton police station? Why weren't the interviews of Morales audio taped or video recorded? This was a cop killing for God sakes! Morales claimed he didn't know the driver of the white car was a cop and MSP said he did know. It was an issue that would loom large.

Morales's version of the incident was marginally believable because just prior to the shooting he had been involved in a fight with a man that was trying to rob him who threatened to come back and, according to what Eddie told me, kill him. Eddie stated to me he believed the man was sent by the former drug dealer on the corner of Walnut and Sargeant Streets called "Gringo." So he sent a runner on a bicycle to his drug supplier, a Hispanic male nicknamed "Flacko," to tell him what happened with the guy in the blue car. Eddie thought Gringo was trying to re-claim his drug territory. In the meantime, a white car came screeching up Sargeant Street and stopped at an angle with the passenger window half way down. Eddie looked into the car and saw a Caucasian man dressed in black. Eddie thought this man was sent by Gringo. Eddie claims he had no clue whatsoever that the driver of this white car was a cop. The driver never identified himself as a cop. The only words he spoke were "stop right there." Eddie saw no emergency lights on or in the vehicle. He knew that the emergency/blue lights would usually be located in the grill of an unmarked police vehicle - on at least the ones that he had seen, which he knew to be wine colored or gray. Morales saw no antennae that would lead him to believe the car was a police car. And when he had previously observed unmarked police cars in the area, two people were in them. In short, Eddie claims he had never before seen a white unmarked police car and was not familiar with it, especially one that looked an awful lot like one of the taxi cab's that were driven around Holyoke.

So Eddie split and the white car began chasing him. Eddie ran up Sargeant Street and took a left turn into an alley. He said he grabbed a gun that was under a dumpster and continued to run down the alley. He then looked back and saw the white car coming down the alley at a fast rate of speed. Eddie was beginning to tire (he weighed two hundred ninety pounds at the time); he had run a considerable distance. Eddie told me that at that point he thought the driver of the car was going to kill him. He continued to run up to the Walnut and Hampshire Street intersection. He heard tires screeching. Eddie said he saw Flacko, his drug supplier, walking up Walnut Street; then he heard two gunshots – "bang, bang." Eddie stated he could not determine where the shots came from because he is deaf in the left ear, but he believed they came from the white car. He stopped running and took the gun out of his waistband. Eddie chambered a round, turned, and started shooting at the white car while moving toward the vehicle. He saw no emergency lights and heard no siren (neither did any eyewitness). His right arm was outstretched and he was holding the gun straight while shooting. Eddie claimed that he did not come to a complete stop during the time he was shooting. After the shooting, Eddie said he jumped a fence and went to Flacko's house where he got rid of the gun. Flacko was waiting for him. He left the gun with Flacko and denied putting it outside on the street in a trash bag. He then went to McDonalds and was picked up by a friend on Appleton Street. He was taken to Troy, NY where he caught a bus to Philadelphia. It was on Christmas day that Eddie met up with his boyhood friend nicknamed "Candle" who would eventually turn him in. Candle then drove Eddie to his home in Scranton, Pennsylvania.

As I said, the Morales defense of self-defense on this tragic homicide case boiled down to simple comments made to police in eight statements. Although I did manage to persuade some of the key witnesses to cooperate with me, it was an experience worse than having a molar root canal. Nobody really wanted to talk to me or anyone else on the defense team. Most of the witnesses were scared to death. Those that weren't didn't want any part of Eddie Morales. The cop's were telling witnesses not to talk to us. The DA's office had people telling witnesses they didn't have to talk to us due to a sequestration order. There was even a time when Rob Diaz and I where at the apartment of the guy that first threatened Morales on Sargeant Street and MSP investigators (Higgins and Soto) miraculously appeared ten minutes after we arrived, stopped our defense interview, and Higgins said to the witness "Do you know who these guys are?" as if we were not entitled. It was a mess. But we didn't stop. There was no quitting, no surrender. I did eventually speak to almost all the witnesses we needed to talk to most, even though the environment was hostile.

But I knew the effort was futile because the degree of force used by Morales was extremely excessive. Peter Ettenberg knew as well. After examining DiNapoli's white car, excessive force became rather obvious as there was a close grouping of six round bullet holes in the passenger side windshield that sent chills cutting through me like a cold northeast wind. It didn't matter if Eddie was being chased. It didn't matter if he was cut off by a vehicle that looked like a cab. It didn't matter if the car blocked his path. It didn't matter whether or not the blue lights and siren were off (although we'll never know what would have happened if they were on). It didn't matter if Eddie felt threatened. It didn't matter whether he did or did not know the operator of the white car was a cop. It just did not matter.

In March of 2001, Eddie Morales was tried in front of TV cameras and a courtroom packed with police, family members and friends of John DiNapoli, and the media. He did not testify. Morales had no one, except Peter Ettenberg and me. He could've had Perry Mason and Paul Drake and it still wouldn't have mattered.

Eddie Morales was found guilty of first-degree murder on March 16, 2001 and sentenced to life in prison without parole. The trial lasted just under ten days. Peter L. Ettenberg did a tremendous job, had the DA and police nervous throughout, and gave a closing argument Clarence Darrow couldn't have made. Eddie never uttered a peep when the verdict was read. He knew it too. When Eddie was in the holding cell right after the verdict he told Ettenberg that he was grateful for everything Peter did for him and for the job we both had done on his behalf. I couldn't believe it. Even in his darkest hour, Eddie Morales was thanking us. I guess it was the first time there had been a John DiNapoli in his life. And that's part of the shame of the whole thing. Had there been a John DiNapoli in the life of Eddie O. Morales prior to December of 1999, I wouldn't be writing about this tragedy, and John DiNapoli would still be alive. I wish it were the case.

The day after the trial, Peter Ettenberg emailed me a personal note:

> *"I want you to know that one of the reasons we put up the fight we did was due to your dogged efforts. You never gave up. You never got discouraged. If a roadblock appeared, you found a way around it. You took a great load off my mind by not having to "think of everything." We're a pretty good team together and I'm grateful for that. I can't tell you how much I appreciate your thoughtful analysis of issues dealing with the investigation and how it all ties together. You clearly are a great PI!! I look forward to MANY more years slugging it out in the trenches with you."*[21]

It just doesn't get any better than this. It's what you want your clients to write to you and about you. I'm simply blessed with the best. And there's no question Peter Ettenberg is the best. No question at all.

In June of 2001, Peter and I would make our first and only public presentation about investigating and defending Eddie Morales at the National Association of Legal Investigators annual conference in Boston. The presentation was titled "Defending the Indefensible" and we told the true story about our experiences. It was heart wrenching for both of us. We've really never spoken about it since. I don't know why; it's not something we planned to do or not do. But I recently asked Peter to comment about his final thoughts on the case as it pertains to the series of uncontrollable events that inexorably unfolded before our very eyes and here's what he had to say:

> *"Anytime you defend someone charged with killing a cop, the stakes get raised a hundred fold. When I added in the feelings that the City of Holyoke had for John DiNapoli, and the composure and class of his daughter, I knew the case would be even more pressure packed. Morales killed him in broad daylight in front of a bunch of witnesses. He led the police on a national manhunt and then was paraded through town like a prized animal. He confessed. It was hopeless but I really felt calm. I knew that somehow we'd come up with a viable defense to make them prove the case in public. I knew there'd never be a deal offered. It was all or nothing from the start and I felt ready for the challenge."*[22]

So when Peter sent that letter asking me to "let him know" what I wanted to do after I reviewed the case, I knew right away he was ready for the challenge. Peter is not one to back down from any challenge. And neither am I, especially when faced with an investigation *against all odds.* We fought the fight and lost a no-win battle. There was no disappointment. Throughout the surreal experience, we held our heads high with honor, character, and integrity. Our pride remained intact. And Sisyphus, the great hero of hope through endless labor, was with us all the way.

United States verses Timothy McVeigh[23]

The cell phone rings while you are in the middle of Thanksgiving Holiday. Shit! It's Dennis Hartley. You listen carefully to what he is saying kind of matter-of-factly! You roll your eyes, swallow hard, and say into the phone "Okay I'll do it." Then you sit back in your chair and wonder what in the hell you just said and why you said it. Reality sets in and you realize you've accepted the case of the century; the case of a lifetime. A thought pops into your mind: "You're now working in the best interest of whom?" The Oklahoma City Bomber? What did I do? Oh my! It should be more like, oh why? It's enough to make anyone want to cry.

Would you take this case on if you had the chance? Would you consider it a golden opportunity or a beast of burden to investigate on behalf of Timothy McVeigh? Why would you want it, especially post conviction? The son of a bitch is guilty...right? It's what's referred to as a "Last Chance" Investigation. It is the ultimate "Sisyphus Syndrome" case. We all know the facts of this case. Timothy McVeigh and Terry Nichols conspired and planned to bomb the Alfred P. Murrah Federal Building in Oklahoma City on April 19, 1995 and McVeigh carried it out. It was, and still is, the single biggest act of domestic terrorism committed by an American: one hundred sixty eight – that's 168 – people killed and many more wounded. McVeigh was tried, convicted, and sentenced to death. It's a miracle he didn't kill himself in the process. More than a few people believe it would've been a lot better if he did and a lot cheaper to the American taxpayer. McVeigh's appeal went on for years until he called his lawyers off. Three months to the day before the 9/11 terrorist attacks on the United States, Timothy McVeigh was put to death at the Federal Penitentiary in Terre Haute, Indiana by lethal injection. Ellis Armistead was there! Ellis Armistead signed for McVeigh's body and took him for a ride. A ride into the history books.

I'm really not interested in conducting high profile federal death penalty investigations, but there are those out there that do nothing else. I just can't imagine taking on an investigation of this significance and magnitude. Although I guess it all depends upon the attorneys you have as clients. If your top attorney client takes on a case of this magnitude and asks you to join the defense team are you going to disappoint the client? I think not. Are you obligated to take the case if you value the relationship you have with this attorney? I think so. Never abandon your clients because you'll lose them in a heartbeat. So if a case like USA v. Timothy McVeigh comes along, take a look at it but don't look too long. If it's an attorney you've never before worked with that comes knocking and there's no loyalty or trust, then it might be best to turn it down unless you are able to get past the trust issues. And don't get sucked into the media hype of the case. PI's don't get rich by writing a book about some high profile case. I accepted, reviewed, signed a protective order, and then eventually turned down the Eric Robert Rudolph case (the Atlanta Olympics and Birmingham, Alabama abortion clinic bomber who was on the lam for five years). Why? I had problems with defense attorneys and they had problems with me (and they're the ones that came a' calling, practically begging); it was a bottom line issue of loyalty and trust. So if there is a loyal and trusting relationship with a valued client and he or she wants you to work a high profile murder case, take it on if you have the know how and wherewithal. But I'd be remiss if I didn't tell you that these cases will consume you; every waking (and even sleeping) moment will be swallowed up by the case. Your life will be the case. Everything else becomes secondary, including your family and the rest of your business. And it can be devastating in more ways than you'll ever know.

H. Ellis Armistead was forty nine years old when he accepted the "last chance" US Code Title 28 Section 2255 death penalty investigation of USA v. Timothy McVeigh. This writ of habeas corpus appeal was based primarily on ineffective assistance of trial counsel in the mitigation (death penalty) investigation and in legal representation prior to McVeigh's trial. Why would any private investigator take on this massive investigation? Was it an effort in futility? Did the defense of Timothy McVeigh waste taxpayer dollars (over $13 million)? Was there closure for the families of the dead, or the wounded? Could there be any measure of satisfaction or resolution gained? I can't answer these questions. But Ellis Armistead can and did answer these questions and many more.

Ellis has done some big ones....Jon Benet Ramsey and Columbine immediately come to mind. But McVeigh changed his life. Ellis has never discussed the case in public. He probably never will. I asked Ellis to share some of his thoughts, opinions, and experiences about the McVeigh death penalty investigation and he agreed to talk to me about it. I asked Armistead to talk about this case because investigation to stop the execution of the biggest American terrorist in United States history has to be the ultimate example of fruitless labor; laborious torture; and investigation *against all odds.* I asked him because he's my friend, a professional colleague, a good man, and a great PI. He could've said no but he didn't.

Right before McVeigh was executed, Ellis Armistead went into the "death house" to talk to him. Ellis had just worked the last nineteen months of his life trying to save a life; not just any life, the life of Timothy McVeigh. But it was not to be. What follows is a question and answer session that took place between Ellis and me:

John: I want to ask you some questions about the McVeigh case?

Ellis: Okay.

John: I don't think you've ever spoken about this case in public before, have you?

Ellis: Not generally, no.

John: How did you get involved in this case?

Ellis: Judge Matsch (federal judge who handled McVeigh's case) appointed Dennis Hartley and Nathan Chambers as McVeigh's attorneys for the purposes of 2255 proceedings (habeas corpus remedies on motion attacking sentence)[24]. Hartley called me over Thanksgiving in, I think, 1999; I was in Seattle, Washington. Hartley says "Judge Matsch wants me to handle the 2255 appeal on McVeigh, would you work on it?"

John: What'd you say?

Ellis: I said okay, I'll do it.

John: That was it? You just said, "I'll do it?"

Ellis: No, not really...I had kind of danced with this before. When the whole bombing went down there were people who had called me and asked me if I'd work on the case. They thought they were gonna get the case and none of them ever did and so I never worked on it until Hartley called. So it wasn't the first time I had been approached about it.

John: Weren't you in some sort of disbelief? After all, it was the single biggest act of domestic terrorism prior to 9/11 in US history; and the biggest committed by a US Citizen.

Ellis: I probably did some thinking afterwards. I could have called him back up and said I changed my mind but I'd worked with Dennis on other death penalty cases. He and I had a client executed about three years earlier. I don't know if McVeigh knew that.

John: Did you wonder after the call what in the hell you just did?

Ellis: Well, I knew I'd jumped into something that was gonna be time consuming. Just by the sheer volume of the file... almost a million pages of discovery. And I knew it wasn't gonna be very popular.

John: How much of that discovery did you actually read?

Ellis: Oh, fifty thousand pages maybe.

John: So you knew the case inside and out?

Ellis: Oh, yeah.

John: I don't think McVeigh ever disputed that he did the bombing, did he?

Ellis: No, he never told me he didn't do it.

John: Did he admit to doing it?

Ellis: I believe so. There were two reporters from Buffalo that kind of had an inside track to him. He supposedly told them he did it.

John: Did McVeigh ever tell you flat-out that he bombed the building?

Ellis: No, I never got into that.

John: You never asked him?

Ellis: No, I didn't care. Well, I cared that people had been hurt and had died, but it didn't really matter to me in doing my job whether he did it or not.

John: Do you believe that Terry Nichols helped him?

Ellis: I think he probably did. It's no wonder these two didn't blow each other up. Just a couple of knuckleheads. It wasn't real sophisticated; fertilizer and jet fuel and a truck to put it in. I mean you just think of two good `ole country boys who used that stuff to blow stumps. That's where they got their idea.

John: Is McVeigh a monster or what?

Ellis: Monster, I don't know. I'm not convinced that when he drove up in front of that building he knew he was going to cause the kind of destruction he did. I mean it's a wonder he didn't blow himself up getting there. It probably couldn't be replicated again. Just probably a freak thing that a fertilizer bomb could do that much damage.

John: So how did he light it?

Ellis: I think from within the cab and I'm not sure if he actually lit it with a match or with a fuse. I really didn't pay much attention to that part of it because I was doing the 2255 investigation.

John: What was that all about?

Ellis: We focused on ineffective assistance of counsel 'cause the original defense team had not given an adequate amount of energy to mitigation issues.

John: Wait a minute; weren't there a slew of lawyers representing McVeigh?

Ellis: At trial, there were twenty eight attorneys on staff. Steven Jones was the primary counsel for

McVeigh at trial. He's a character. Jones and his people promoted their own personal goals and agendas above McVeigh's.

John: Do you mean in the media.

Ellis: Yeah.

John: So Jones wanted to get famous?

Ellis: Yeah, flying around the world.

John: Wow, twenty eight attorneys...

Ellis: And Rob Nigh was one of them.

John: McVeigh wanted to get famous too, didn't he?

Ellis: A lot of these guys like to talk to the press. They're narcissistic. I found out quickly that McVeigh, through the years since his arrest, had developed a network of reporter friends, informants if you will. He was a sly guy and he played people off against each other, including the attorneys.

John: Really?

Ellis: He knew a lot about what was going on. And he knew how to manipulate people.

John: So about your investigation, were you the only one working on it at the time?

Ellis: Well, people from my office.

John: Who?

Ellis: Me, Jennifer Getty, Connie Lindsay, Jim Walton, and Karen Myers. They spent two or three months of time out in Oklahoma just copying files.

John: Did the case consume you?

Ellis: Yup, pretty much; for a couple of years.

John: What did you and your people do?

Ellis: We supported the appeal attorney's 2255 theories. We spoke to the trial attorneys and trial investigators. The trial investigators did a fairly good job considering what they had to work with. I'm not sure how good a direction they were given by Steve Jones. We also spoke with the families of the victims too.

John: All one hundred sixty eight of them?

Ellis: No, selected ones.

John: Why selected?

Ellis: Ones that we knew were most apt to speak with us, the ones that's were a bit more vocal.

John: Did any of them oppose putting McVeigh to death?

Ellis: There was one guy, I forget his name, you'd see him in the literature; his daughter was killed. Not many were opposed.

John: How many interviews did you do?

Ellis: A lot, I don't remember how many.

John: And what were you asking family members?

Ellis: Did they think that McVeigh should be executed, mainly. Some of them were afraid if he was executed too soon that a lot of secrets would die.

John: What secrets?

Ellis: McVeigh's secrets.

John: Did you talk to any of the victim's that lived?

Ellis: We concentrated mostly on the families of the victims that died.

John: Did they all talk to you?

Ellis: Some of them would, some wouldn't.

John: Did you interview McVeigh?

Ellis: Yes, I met with him dozens of times. Generally, when one of the attorneys went to meet with him, I would go. I got to know him fairly well. I liked him. He was easy to get along with and didn't cause any problems. I knew his family. His father, Bill, is a nice guy, a really solid guy. His younger sister, Jennifer, is a bright, attractive, articulate schoolteacher, but suspicious of everybody. I never met his mother or older sister.

John: You say McVeigh's father was a nice, really solid guy, but what about Tim McVeigh? What kind of guy was he?

Ellis: He was a decent guy.

John: He was?

Ellis: As long as you didn't talk politics. He hated the government.

John: Why?

Ellis: Waco and that kind of stuff. He talked a lot about Waco.

John: So the motive for the bombing was Waco?

Ellis: Just government hate.

John: Was there any hope for sparing McVeigh's life?

Ellis: There's always hope, but.... You get a little hope and then you figure out what you're dealing with. It's kind of as in every murder trial you think you have some hope. Then you get a little thing called trial psychosis. During the 2255 investigation, we'd get a promising lead; it wouldn't pan out and there would be some squirrel (messing things up in the case)... or the attorney's would think they'd have a good issue or hearing and it would fall through the cracks... the judge wouldn't even have a hearing.

John: So did you ever feel like that guy rolling the stone up the hill?

Ellis: Oh, all the time!

John: Did you ever have a chance?

Ellis: Probably not realistically. I don't think Tim meant to kill all those kids, although he really didn't help his cause when he described them as collateral damage.

John: Did you see McVeigh's family before the execution?

Ellis: About three weeks before the execution, I went up to see his father and told him that Tim was gonna be executed.

John: What did Bill say when you told him?

Ellis: He said, "I love my son but I also believe in the death penalty."

John: Wow!

Ellis: It was pretty sad.

John: Did Bill see Tim after you told him Tim was going to be executed?

Ellis: Yeah, I believe Bill and Jennifer went down there (Terre Haute) a couple of weeks before his execution. That was the last time they saw him.

John: When was the last time you saw him?

Ellis: The day he was executed?

John: Did you see it happen?

Ellis: No.

John: Where were you when it happened?

Ellis: I was next door in a trailer.

John: Did you speak to McVeigh that day?

Ellis: Right before the execution, I went into the death house with a deputy coroner and spoke briefly with McVeigh. He was in the holding cell right next to the death chamber. I was there to take the body after the execution. I was also a witness to McVeigh's physical appearance so that someone on the defense team could say he wasn't beaten or injured.

John: What did you say to him?

Ellis: How are you doing?

John: What did he say to you?

Ellis: He said "okay." Then BOP (Bureau of Prisons) officers led me out. Thirty minutes later I was brought back in. And there he was; he was dead. I signed a receipt for his body.

John: Who decided you were going to take the body?

Ellis: It was a team decision. The concern that the family and McVeigh had was that people were offering money for parts of him and we wanted to make sure that we didn't have that problem.

John: What happened after you signed for the body?

Ellis: We put him in a little minivan and rode over to some shop area in the prison complex where we then transferred him to another minivan. McVeigh was in a body bag and we put him in the back of the van.

John: How did you get him off the grounds without the press following you?

Ellis: I hired a decoy hearse that left the penitentiary after the execution. I don't know what it had in it, but it wasn't McVeigh. Then we left with McVeigh in the minivan right along with all the employees at the shift change.

John: Where did you bring him after you left the penitentiary?

Ellis: We drove around town for about an hour because someone had tipped off the press to the mortuary we were going to use (to cremate McVeigh). There was this deputy U.S. Marshall riding with us; he kept talking on his radio and I said, look, lets just get this done; I don't want to have a wreck or run out of gas with this dead guy here. It was my decision, I guess, since he was in my custody so we just went to the mortuary. We pulled in there and Jennifer Getty was waiting on me. Then we just got him fired up.

John: McVeigh was cremated?

Ellis: Right. His ashes were put in an urn.

John: Any press at the mortuary?

Ellis: Yeah, they were standing outside. They didn't follow us when we left the mortuary.

John: What did you do with the urn?

Ellis: We just took it with us. We went to Indianapolis. When we got to Indianapolis, Jennifer took the urn and put him in her backpack.

John: What did you do next?

Ellis: We spent the night and then got on a plane.

John: Did Jennifer still have the urn in her backpack on the plane?

Ellis: Right.

John: Did she have any problems with airport security?

Ellis: No.

John: So Jennifer carried the urn back to Denver and McVeigh was in her backpack as a carry on item?

Ellis: Yeah.

John: What did you do with the urn?

Ellis: I kept it in my evidence locker for about a year until I turned him over to one of the attorneys.

John: Do you know if the family has the ashes?

Ellis: I don't know. I don't even want to know. They may be at sea for all I know. There are all these rumors that they were gonna dump him in Memorial Pond and I just didn't want to know anything about what was going on with him.

John: How did the case affect your business?

Ellis: I think in the long run, it wasn't worth it. I know it wasn't worth it from a financial point. What happens is you have a large client and you're forced to let other client relationships slide ...your bread and butter stuff. I couldn't stay on top of everything. So I think in the long run from a business perspective I'd have been better off without it.

John: How did it affect your private life?

Ellis: There was some strain, you know, with some of my friends who didn't understand why the government was paying me to work on the McVeigh case. I'm not sure I lost them, but it strained me being gone a lot, and strained my marriage. I mean I've always been gone a lot, but this was a little more intense. I think it's taken several years off my life.

John: So there's no question you were profoundly impacted by working this case?

Ellis: It was bizarre....it was bizarre down to the end.

John: Would you do it again?

Ellis: Yeah, I'd do it again. I think it's just one of those things you do. Someone's got to do it. I thought I was qualified to do it. I had been down this road with a client that was executed before and it wasn't something I was just gonna push off onto my employees or someone else.

John: The US taxpayers paid in excess of thirteen million dollars for the defense of this case. Would thirty million dollars have made any difference?

Ellis: I don't think that any amount of money would have made a difference in the outcome.

You know what? I don't think so either; in the McVeigh case or the Morales case. And there's many more cases out there just like them - *against all odds*; where the evidence is so overwhelming the inevitable guilty verdict is staring you in the face even before the defense investigation gets started. It's people like us and the lawyers we work for that protect the constitutional rights of the accused and the convicted. To protect the constitutional rights of any person is advancing the cause of democracy, no matter what the crime. Can you imagine if it was any other way? I can't. But I do know one thing: I don't ever want to find out.

14
I NEED A PI

Character is like a tree and reputation like its shadow. The shadow is what we think of it; the tree is the real thing!

Abraham Lincoln

"Coming to your office is like having to go to the vet to put my dog down." I'll never forget these words. It's what a client said after he hired me to conduct an investigation on a longtime colleague and valued employee. He didn't want to do it but knew he had to. And that's how ninety five percent of private clients feel and think when they are hiring a PI; the other five percent either don't care or actually thrive on it. When I say private clients, I'm not talking about insurance companies and law firms. I'm talking about the average Joe or Josephine that calls you because they have a problem that needs to be fixed. I'm talking about the small business owner that has a problem employee; I'm talking about the female college professor that is being stalked by her student but police are unable or unwilling to help her; I'm talking about a dad that is experiencing life with a sixteen year old son who is dealing drugs; I'm talking about a wife that knows her marriage is over because her hubby of twenty years is having an affair with her own best friend; I'm talking about the father of two small children whose drug addicted ex wife is falsely alleging abuse, and custody of the children is in question; I'm talking about the parents of a missing daughter; I'm talking about a judge that has serious family issues; I'm talking about the man who is feuding with his neighbor; I'm talking about the mother and father of a loved son who was killed in a horrific auto accident or was a victim of an unsolved homicide; and I could go on forever with example after example of vexing real life problems. What's not so shocking to me, and could some day come true, is I could be talking about you.

Most people that call or meet with a PI for consultation are usually having a first-time experience with a problem they cannot solve themselves; or the problem is long standing and someone finally feels compelled to do something about it. These potential clients have probably never met with or talked to a private investigator about their particular problem in a business setting; no doubt they are perplexed. Sometimes they don't know if they actually need a PI, an attorney, a shrink, or a combination thereof. They may already have an attorney, but many times they do not. I find that there are three common denominators with potential private clients: they need someone to really listen to them; they need a plan; and they need to be reassured. They hope for the best. I prepare them for the worst. They expect miracles. I tell them there are no guarantees. They want an end result. I tell them it may not turn out to be the result they want. They want one price for investigation. I ask them if they have thought about a budget. They still want a price. I give them a range. But what they want most they almost never ask about, and that is peace of mind. Perhaps they know I can't really assist them in this area. But I still tell them I can almost always help them if an investigation is necessary; I give no assurance as to the outcome. And what about peace of mind! Well, it's usually heartache we're dealing with and not peace. If some semblance of peace is eventually realized then the client gains a psychological benefit from the successful resolution of the investigation; and that's great because they did something about it and felt like they were part of it. What I'm more interested in doing is solving the client's problem to help them make decisions. And so, more times than not, peace may not surface even though the problem is resolved or solved. Buyer beware.

The necessity of investigation. Some people have no idea as to whether or not their problem warrants an investigation until the PI consultation. Most people who have a problem that needs to be investigated know the investigation is necessary before the consultation because they themselves have decided private investigation is necessary or someone has told them it's necessary. In most cases, an attorney, friend, business associate, or relative has made the suggestion of hiring a private investigator to help solve the problem. The conclusion: *"I need a PI."* Then the initial consultation follows once a potential client figures out whom to hire.

Not every problem needs to be investigated though. For instance, infidelity in a divorce case in the Commonwealth of Massachusetts is really not an issue in this "no fault" divorce state. No fault divorce means neither party blames the other for the breakdown in the marriage; thus the behavior of either party cannot be used in determining asset distribution. So, conducting investigation on infidelity to support or bolster a divorce action in Massachusetts is worthless and unnecessary for court purposes. Yet in Massachusetts, surveillance investigation followed by background investigation is entirely appropriate and necessary in issues of child custody where the opposing spouse is seeking custody of the children in a divorce but thought to be keeping the company of an individual convicted of, let's say, some act of pedophilia. What judge would allow kids to be around a convicted sex offender? So an investigation would be considered reasonable and necessary in order to prove that the opposing spouse is allowing the children to be in the company of a sex offender.

In most private client cases, investigation is warranted if there is a legitimate legal or logical reason for it. If not, I tend to stay away from them. If there is a legal issue over and beyond any investigative concern, I always tell the potential client to hire an attorney and then assess investigation needs. PI's are not lawyers and should never provide legal advice. So the client screening process becomes an important factor as a potential client's need may dictate something other than you can provide.

Who to hire. Who do potential private clients hire? Of course I want them all to hire me! No... seriously, I want to service only those clients that want me to work their case, are comfortable with my staff and me, and can afford to pay me. I'm much too busy to wine and dine potential clients. Glad-handing is not something I do well; I'm terrible at it. Besides, if you *have to* wine and dine clients to get their business, including insurance company adjusters and attorneys, what does that say about the quality of your work? I let the quality of the work and my reputation do the talking. And so should you. If you're new in this business, establish your reputation through hard work, honesty, and integrity. I did. I'm still doing it. It's what separates and distinguishes you from the rest of the crowd. It forms your character and defines your unique talents and style. Private clients should hire a competent, cost effective, local PI. They should also feel comfortable with the selection. It's incumbent upon you to make them feel comfortable with their decision.

The local PI is always better. The local private investigator with a good solid reputation in the area where the investigation will take place is the one to find. Local PI's know the geographic area, the people, always have the better sources in their area, and are familiar with the local customs and traditions of the local people. They know the state and local court system, police departments, hospitals, public record custodians, and politicians much better than the outsider PI. Look hard because competent, expert local PI's are difficult to find. They are out there and you can find them, but it takes hard work, research, and time.

There are at least four exceptions to hiring a local PI:

1) Very sensitive, extremely confidential, complex, and high profile cases might be best left with the specialist PI. For instance, even though the Holyoke, MA cop killer case was outside of my local area in the County of Hampden (I am more comfortable in Worcester, Middlesex, Norfolk, and Suffolk counties), I was retained to conduct the defense investigation. The case was extremely high profile and sensitive. The defense needed a specialist in self-defense homicide investigation and I had the working knowledge and expertise in self-defense cases. Over a long period of time, I had consistently established a reputation as an aggressive, determined, practical, and hard working PI with the right expert connections; it's what

the case needed. I was also well known as a competent case manager and organizer. And last, defense counsel Peter Ettenberg was from my area, had worked with me extensively on other murder cases, and wanted me to lead the defense investigation. I'm grateful he selected me.

2) If the preferred PI agency has a staff of investigators covering areas in addition to their home locality, it may make sense to the client to have a familiar case manager managing the investigation and a staff investigator local and accustomed to the geography in which the investigation is situated conducting the field work.

3) The preferred PI or PI agency has superior case management and organization skills. As an example, if there's a case in a state like Florida, for instance, or any other state outside my licensed area in which a client wants me to work because they believe I'm a competent, superior case manager, I'll take the case and find the most efficient local licensed investigator to do the fieldwork. This frequently happens with business clients such as insurance companies and big corporations. I've done cases all over the country and abroad by locating competent local investigators and sub contracting the field work while managing the overall case investigation. I've traveled to other states and countries and worked with local licensed PI's. It's great. I get to know, work with, and develop friendships with competent local PI's all over the world. It also benefits my agency because I receive many referral case investigations in Massachusetts because I am known outside of my local area. When a familiar out of state investigator needs an investigator in Massachusetts, he or she calls me or refers a client my way.

4) If the client cannot find a competent investigator in the area where investigation is needed, then it becomes necessary to hire a preferred non-local PI. It happens more than you think. Still, the hired non-local PI must

comply with the local licensing requirements so a local PI may be hired anyway. The local PI can help out when needed, but usually does not play a significant role in the investigation. I flat-out refuse to hire an out of state investigator that cannot get the job done and do it well. I'd rather travel and do the work myself. Character and reputation play a rather large role in the selection process of local investigators in states, or other jurisdictions, where you need investigation. And competence is the key. Sometimes you can't get what you need so you must find the PI best suited to satisfy your needs with the ability to get the job done right, no matter where he or she is located.

The best is not always best. "I want the best!" I hear this a lot. And I see a lot of potential PI clients get caught up in trying to determine who the best private investigator out there is, especially people with money to spare. They want the best, even though the best may not be best for them. It's nearly impossible to determine who the best PI is; best in what? There are veritable, competent, expert PI's out there that specialize in various kinds of investigation. The client needs to identify and consult with one or two of them to determine who best fits their needs. They'll know when they have the PI that is right for them.

How to identify a competent local PI. It takes work. Research is the best bet. Check out state and national PI association websites, local PI websites by Internet browser searches, the phone book, attorney references, and the local courthouse. Ask around. Once you get the name of a PI, make a phone call and screen the PI. A competent PI will always encourage the potential client to check out their credentials with local and state licensing authorities, local attorneys, the Chamber of Commerce, Better Business Bureau, the Small Business Administration, and verifying agencies such as the local police department and the local courthouse. Good, reputable, and competent local PI's have nothing to hide and a client to gain so they should be willing to point you in the right direction to check on credentials. If not, then it is usually a sign that something is wrong. Although I wouldn't rely on police to make a determination on the competence of a private sector investigator, I would check to see if a PI has had problems with local police or the public; a local PI might be known to the police and it's always worth a phone call to the chief or department representative. Always check the local courts to see if the PI has a criminal and civil history. There is nothing more telling than a PI that has been sued a number of times or has a history of arrests. But also be advised that PI's can be sued for frivolous matters and wrongfully accused. If there is an extended civil or criminal history with a PI, I would tend to stay away from hiring this person to work for me or anyone else. A potential client should always ask the PI for existing client references and take a long hard look at the PI's website and office. It doesn't take much to determine who is financially successful. And usually, but not always, financial success has a lot to do with competence. Perhaps the best indicator of a successful and competent local PI is reputation within the legal community. Calling a few reputable attorneys in the local area and asking about a particular PI may yield results. But it still comes down to comfort and trust. That's why PI's should have a working office in which to meet clients. Virtual offices and mail drops are second rate. Meeting clients at third party locations is not desirable either. It's just my opinion, but any client that turns over a few hundred to a few thousand dollars or more to a PI they just met in a restaurant is a fool. But it happens all the time. Then when the hired PI isn't making contact with the client, doesn't do the work as promised, or has taken the money and run, where does the client go? I'll tell you what – not to another PI. Yikes!

Business clients are looking for value. Although private clients are usually looking for competence, quality, and value, business clients are searching for mostly value in PI services. I have had business clients think they can get the same quality investigation done for $45.00 per hour as opposed to paying $75.00 or $100.00 per hour. I have news for them: *no way!* The old adage "you get what you pay for" is especially true in the PI profession. There'll always be the overpriced PI as I've already discussed. But for the most part, the competent, well established PI can and will charge big bucks. The client should be expected to pay the price for excellent services and superior competence. Good business clients will want to pay less per hour for loyalty to the PI agency, repeat business, and long-standing profitable relationships. There is nothing wrong with this kind of business. In fact, it's good business. Look to establish long lasting business relationships with insurance companies, corporations, law firms, and other business entities. Lower your hourly rate about fifteen to twenty percent in exchange for steady work from these dedicated and loyal clients. They need PI's as much as we need them. Let there be no mistake about it.

I hope no one has had to put his dog down to get a feel for what it's like to visit my office and hire me. I assure you, I won't make any client feel quite that bad. I don't think it was me, anyway, so I'm not too worried about the analogy. What this job is all about is the client. It's not about me, and it's not about you. It's about helping people; helping people to make important decisions in their lives and in the lives of loved ones. Quality of life is what matters. And it's vitally important to realize that you are part of defining the quality of life for people who place great trust and dependency on you and your investigative acumen.

It's a balancing act. So don't fall! And always remember that truth is sometimes stranger than fiction[25].

15
A BALANCING ACT

I have simply tried to do what seemed best each day, as each day came.

Abraham Lincoln

I have this recurring dream. The setting is a circus. The main tent is packed. People are going nuts outside but it is deadly quiet in the tent. The scene turns to a man on a tightrope high in the sky but under the top of the tent. He's on the rope just past midpoint. There is no net underneath! The sweet smell of popcorn permeates the air. Everyone is looking up, holding their breath. Not a soul is moving. The man is walking on the rope, arms stretched east and west. Carefully and swiftly, the man puts one foot in front of the other occasionally stopping to settle himself. The picture zooms to the walker but the face is out of focus. I struggle to maintain the dream but it is fading fast. The last thing I see is his face. Surprisingly, I'm not shocked. The tightrope walker is me. I wake up but there is no panic, no sweat. I shake it off. I have to get up 'cause I'm feeling dizzy. I put my foot out to touch the floor in the still of darkness. I am relieved when my foot touches something solid. I stand up and let out a long sigh. I'm safe. I wipe the sockets of my eyes with my thumb and forefinger. Wow! What a dream. It has never finished; I doubt it ever will. I pray it never does. I no longer attempt to interpret this dream because, as best as I can determine, the dream is my life; *a balancing act.*

Tell you the truth, I'd much rather be the juggler; even the man that swallows fire. I now try to stay away from the circus at all costs. About as close as I get to a real circus when I'm not working is at the Sterling Fair in my hometown of Sterling, Massachusetts. And thank God it only comes around once a year. But at least I'm safe there. There is no tightrope. And I'm with my family. I see my friends and my kids' friends. My mind is on everything *but* investigation. My attentions are with my children and on my wife; they are definitely not at the circus; the circus I call work. And I try to repeat this activity in some capacity, at some place and point, each and every week. It's how I survive on any particular weekend. It's how my family life survives. It's how my marriage survives. It's how my business survives. It's how my sanity survives. It's how my life survives.

I do not want life to come around and kick me good on the backside. Life is much too short to spend working all the time. But the demands on time are mind boggling in the private investigation business, particularly if you own an investigation agency. It's hard to explain, but sometimes it seems as if there is no start time and no end time when I'm at work. At times, it feels as though one day blends in with the next, and the next, and then the next. Other times no. It is a euphemism to say that time management is big! You must balance your time.

You must have balance in your life. Balance is extremely important because too much of one thing can spoil you to death, and I do mean death. Too much of anything will end up killing you. It's like the tightrope walker, too much force in any one direction and....well, you know what happens then. So let's discuss the balance every private investigator should try to achieve at work, with family and friends, while alone, and in play. I can only speak for myself and about my observations. I've been on the tightrope for more than just a few years and I haven't fallen...yet! I've had some close calls more times than I care to discuss, but to fall....not quite yet. I'm thankful. I pray I can manage to make it across. I hope you do to.

In order to have balance, you must have focus. In order to focus on a particular problem, situation, or matter, you must reduce stress, not worry about other concerns, and concentrate in order to allow the brain *to* focus. Once the brain is focused, you can balance.

You cannot focus or balance if you do not take care of yourself physically and mentally. Take care of yourself and you'll be able to care for others. Love yourself and you'll be able to love others. Be yourself and you'll be comfortable with others. And the opposite holds true as well. You must understand how to focus concentration on areas of life that matter and pay little attention to those things that are of little or no consequence. Only you can search for that understanding and the answer that allows it to happen for you. The trick is to find the answer that is best suited for you and everyone around you. You find the answers as you experience life.

The first thing I do to protect me when I'm on the tightrope is to have a safety net if I fall. Always set up the net to catch you if you fall. Have a support system in place. Just as the business is a support system for my family, my family is a support system for me. They must believe in you. If you ignore them, they will ignore you. If you love them, they will love you. If you pay attention to them, they will pay attention to you. If you support them, they will support you. It must be this way or you cannot have balance, much less happiness. Your main support system should be your family, then your work, followed by your close friends. If it's any other way, adjust your priorities or do what it takes to get back into balance.

In order to support family, friends, and loved ones, you must give them time. And time is a precious commodity. Most people take advantage of it early in life and lament about it at the end. Try to avoid this if you can. In any event, I make time for my family and friends (even if at times they do not make time for me). You must take the time to make time. No excuses. The problems will still be at work when you return to the office. One problem is replaced by another, and then another, and so it goes. So nothing is more important than making time for the things that are important in life: Family, work, friends, self; in that order. Everything else is back burner stuff and time should be allocated to allow for it. So let's discuss time and try to define it as follows:

Quality time: Who in the hell conjured up this cliché? I have to believe it was some yuppie driving a Volvo in the late eighties for sure. It was repeated ad nauseum as if it had deep meaning: "I've got to spend some *quality time* with my family" or "I spent some *quality time* with my friends this weekend." Let me tell you right now: All time is *quality time* and it must be treated as such. Time is time. It's just that simple. Now it is true that the things you experience in time can be good, bad, indifferent, exciting, boring, puzzling, mysterious, and so forth. Don't confuse time with experience. And don't blame time for your experience. Time is valuable but it's not a quality. Your experience is what determines quality; not of time, but of life. Remember, it is quality of life that matters. Although time is a good healer after a bad experience if you allow it to be, don't wish your life away. It doesn't last that long anyway.

Family time: Family time is the most important time, not work time or any other time. You must make time for your family or you'll find yourself without them one day wondering what the hell happened and where you went wrong. It can be very lonely out there without your family. Lose your family and you lose a large part of your support system. Try losing your balance with a weakened support system. It'll be much harder to recover. It's especially true for investigators because support from other sources such as friends and work may not be enough. I try to have my family understand my work. So I've asked them to become involved in the business. But it's their decision, not mine. They are not obligated and no pressure to favor one workplace over the next is applied by "Daddio." My children are told they must experience work at some point after they turn fourteen. My wife wanted to learn a new trade after fifteen years in the medical profession. She was sick of working holidays. I'm thankful she chose my business. I am thankful my two older kids chose it as well for summer work. Where else can they go to assure and arrange adequate time off for a family summer vacation and an occasional time out here and there? My wife and kids work hard. They are paid and paid accordingly, just the same as I would pay any non-family member. My wife is my office manager and a good investigator as well. She works full time and has for the last five years. My son Jason, age eighteen, works for my agency in spring, summer, and fall as a part-time surveillance investigator. He's smart, caught on quickly, and works with diligence and dignity. My sixteen year old daughter Jessica could type over one hundred words per minute accurately when she was fourteen (I lose balance by merely listening to the keyboard hum). So I asked her to come into the office to type part time. She was reluctant at first, but agreed to give it a try. Now she loves it. She's got intelligence, wit, social skills, and is street smart. I think she might turn into a great investigator as well, but only if she wants it. My youngest daughter, Jackie, keeps us intrigued and never complains about mom, dad, brother or sister working at the office. She knows where the bread is buttered, even at age nine. Smart girl. My children are not consumed by the business, but get enough of it to understand me. I get to see them more. They get paid. They learn how to work. It's a win-win situation. And we've become closer because of it. Our family time experiences away from work are fabulous. My kids are intensely involved in school and extracurricular activities. I don't know how they do it. I attend all their functions. I'm involved in their lives. And so is my wife. Show them you care and your family time will be your release and a great joy. Your life will take on much more meaning. Take time away from them and it'll come back to haunt you at a time when you need them most. Your happiness and life balance depends upon a good relationship with family and if you think it doesn't affect your interaction at work and with friends, think again. A family that plays together stays together. Try it; it can and does work out.

Work time: When you're at work, work. And work hard! The success of any business is directly related to hard work. Good life balance requires a need to be productive in a working environment. The experiences at work help you move forward on the tightrope and in life. You'll feel useful if you are helping others, solving real life problems, and contributing to the economic welfare of your community, your employer, and yourself. It's no different when you're working for an investigation agency.

Focusing on your investigative assignments at work enables you to help others by working those cases to a successful conclusion. Staying busy at work is extremely important. Time passes quickly when you're busy as opposed to being idle. Setting daily goals and achieving those goals gives you a sense of purpose and meaning. If you don't have enough work because it happens to be a slow time at your company, take it upon yourself to ask a co-worker if they need assistance; work on long standing marketing projects; call clients to say hello and let them know you're looking for additional business; or ask your boss how you can help out. You also might want to request vacation or a few days off when business is slow. There are cyclical slow periods in the private investigation business just as in many other professions (usually over the holiday periods and when most people take vacation or time off in the summer months). Thank God they don't last long. I use these times to market new clients, catch up on administrative matters, assess and upgrade office equipment and supplies, and to plan and organize short and long term goals. I find something to do to move forward. There is no time to stand still or work in a vacuum. I consider myself lucky, but you make your own luck. Isn't it amazing that the harder you work, the luckier you get? Some people confuse luck and success. Although there is a direct correlation between the two, I'd much rather be successful than be lucky. Hard work will get you there. So during the time you are working, work hard and do what needs to be done to complete your investigations with professional acumen and within established deadlines. You'll be helping others and yourself. Simultaneously, you're making money and maintaining balance while moving forward on the circus tightrope.

Friend time: How many friends do you really have? What is your definition of friendship? How much time are you spending with friends? Stop for a moment and give these questions some serious thought. I can count my truest friends on both sets of fingers; some can count them on one set; and some can't count them at all. I classify friends in three groups: true friends; casual friends; and acquaintances. All three types of friendships can be related to business and/or be personal. True friends are the hardest to develop but are the most rewarding, meaningful, and satisfying. Casual friendships are wonderful and can be long or short term social delights. Only a few true friendships evolve from the many casual friends one develops. Acquaintances are those friends you see and know but with whom you do not really spend much time. And isn't time a key factor in any friendship? It takes much time and effort to maintain a true friendship if you're lucky enough to experience such a relationship. You must give time to your friends. Your friends must give time to you. It's a two-way street. If it doesn't happen, you lose the intensity of the friendship over time. But do not ignore time responsibilities you must devote to your immediate family, your significant other, and your work in order to develop and maintain friendships with those who are less important to your quality of life. You'll quickly upset the balance of your life if you do. Friendships are wonderful and one of life's great treasures. One who is without friends is missing the pleasures and delights of life. Balance is hard to maintain without friends to share your thoughts, feelings, ideas, and experiences. Friendships outside of the investigative arena are sometimes difficult for PI's to develop and maintain. Most people naturally shy away from detectives for reasons that are obvious. Detectives, PI's, legal investigators, and so forth are sometimes wrongfully presumed to be busy bodies, nosey, slimy, dirty, uncaring, and a few choice other words I loath to mention. Select fiction novels, television, and the movie industry has created a negative image of the profession that is almost impossible to overcome. It's getting better as investigators unite to educate the public, lawmakers, and others as to just what it is we actually do, but it's far from perfect. In fact, the image of the American PI is misunderstood. Most PI's are wrongfully maligned and often vilified. The truth is we have been victimized over time by a few bad apples in the bushel. So it goes to follow that private investigators have a tough time developing friendships. Not a lot of people invite us PI-types to cocktail parties. It's a part of life that I've learned to accept. I've overheard the whispers and they aren't usually worth repeating. Work hard to overcome the "gumshoe" negative image and you'll eventually find valuable friendships that will be lasting. Become involved in community activities, sports, music, and social events and you'll make friends. Don't be a loner, isolating and insulating yourself from people who can become your friends and acquaintances. The balancing act will be much more enjoyable with meaningful friendships. While you develop friendships with people from all walks of life, you'll also be advancing the positive image of the profession. And that's a laudable balancing act for sure.

Alone time: I can hear it now from wives, husbands, significant others, sons and daughters, and friends too: "What! You want to be alone! Why would you want that? What can you possibly do alone that you can't do with me? Are you hiding something? If you are, it had better be for me? If you're cheating on me I'll kill you!" The third degree could last a lifetime. Why is it so difficult for some people to understand that other people may want or need to be alone? There is a difference between being alone and being lonely. You must be able to recognize the difference. There are times when you'll need to get away to be alone and to be left alone. Wanting to spend time alone to get to know oneself is normal and healthy. And there is also a difference between being a "loner" and wanting to be alone. Did you ever wonder about people that are never alone, don't like to be alone, go to great lengths to avoid being alone, and are actually scared to be left alone? I have come to the conclusion that these people must not like themselves very much and so they don't want to be left alone with their own self. It's quite sad when someone doesn't like himself to the extent that being alone will cause panic attacks or bizarre, even criminal, behavior. I've seen it happen. It is as equally sad when people are withdrawn to a point that being alone is the norm and hermitic behavior sets in. And so there must be a balance between these two unhealthy behaviors.

Realizing that man is both a social *and* private being is critical. To experience life is to experience people, places, and things. To experience life is to also be private and alone. You're born into the world alone and you leave the world alone. It's real and it's natural. So at times you need to be alone to learn about yourself, to learn to like and love yourself, and to be yourself. You cannot love others until you learn to love yourself, but I won't get romantic, at least not here. The joy of being alone is no different for investigators. In fact, investigators need to watch out that they don't spend too much time alone and spiral out of balance. PI's usually work alone, so they have much time to learn about themselves as well as the subject of their investigations. But to clear the mind completely, work must not enter the equation. Investigators must take time away from family, work, and friends to have alone time. The degree of necessary alone time is determined by the individual. I know I sometimes lock myself in a room, sit down, relax, shut my eyes, and clear my thoughts. I'm then refreshed after this experience. Sometimes I travel alone. I write alone; I research alone; I exercise alone; and I read alone. It doesn't take much alone time to come to understand oneself and feel satisfied, but I believe it's absolutely necessary to have alone time to maintain your balance at work, at home, with friends, and in life. Don't let anybody talk you out of it. The man on the tightrope is certainly alone. So be sure to make the time to be alone so that when you're on the rope you'll know how to handle it.

Playtime: I love playtime! It is undoubtedly a favorite kind of time. You ask why? Probably not what you think; I didn't say party time, although I like that time too. Play time allows my mind to completely focus on what I'm doing without interference from work time thoughts; and the amazing thing about it is.... it's effortless. During playtime, the mind should be so engaged in what it is doing that distractions cannot cause a wandering thought. It happens with ease and can last more than several hours. The trick is to find something you love to do that makes you happy and do it frequently. For example, I founded a classic rock and roll band with two good friends in 2001, Scott Mitchell and David Rose, both superb musicians. Just about every Sunday, and sometimes Tuesday, evening we get together in the rock and roll studio at Lajoie Investigations. Yes, the conference and storage room at the office turns into a music hall with seven musicians going full tilt. It's awesome, complete with electric drums, Korg keyboards, saxophones, guitars galore, and a kick ass sound system. The name of the band is called "Generation Gap" because three of the musicians are teenagers (and these kid's can play) and the four adults are all over forty. We introduce the teens to classic rock and roll ....the Beatles, Chicago, Billy Joel, Spiral Staircase, Pink Floyd, Frankie

Valli, and more. We even do some Gershwin and Brubek too. When I am able to make music, all other thoughts in my mind leave me. I'm refreshed after it happens. We even do paid gigs. It's great. But the amazing thing about it is I don't even think about work when I'm jamming, and I'm doing it at the office. And it feels good!

Playtime should afford your mind the ability to dismiss all the problems and headaches of life and focus on the play at hand. Your troubles disappear for a few hours, even days; a respite from the circus, just as in alone time except you are usually with other people during playtime. But it can be done while you're alone as well. There is one simple rule to follow: Playtime must also be fun time. You must have fun doing it because that's what play time is all about – pure and simple – having fun, doing something that brings great enjoyment outside of work time. All investigators, including law enforcement, need to have playtime. It is a time to let loose in a productive, non-violent way. For me, it's music, vacation, golf, skiing, bike riding, reading, and cooking. For others it can be going to the movies, hiking, rugby, baseball, football, playing pool, swimming, boating, fishing, and so forth... you get the idea. The main purpose of playtime is to have fun; its secondary purpose is to occupy the mind long enough so when you return to work you are refreshed and ready to solve problems. Investigators are dealing with complicated real life problems out on the front lines. It's tough out there. Work a double homicide and see how much fun you'll have – not much, not any! Work a fire loss, a fraud case, a DUI, a surveillance, a child custody matter; locate a deadbeat dad; find a missing child; solve a theft investigation; investigate drug transactions; discover hidden assets; and I could go on and on. Investigative work is not fun. Investigative work is not play. Although it can be satisfying, invigorating, and stimulating, investigation is serious business. It's sometimes simple, but mostly complex. It can be frustrating as well. Not all cases are solved. Not all investigators get to experience the desired end result. You cannot be everything to everybody. I wish it were that easy. All work time and no play time is not good in this business. It's not good in any business but especially in the business of investigation. Balance will quickly spin out of control without getting away for some playtime. So resign yourself to the notion that you'll need to get away to play. Playtime improves your balance and can catch you when losing balance. Be sure to dedicate the time to play. It'll improve the quality of your life at work, at home, with friends, and when you are alone. Your sanity depends upon it. And so does the sanity of others.

Epilogue

My mind is consumed by the dream. I get back in bed after a short respite. I'm wide-awake. My wife is sleeping. No one to talk to; perhaps it is best. The dream is still vivid. I can't shake it. It takes a long time to fall back to sleep. The dream does not return. I'm awakened in the morning by the light. I'm refreshed. I recall the dream and strive to remember its end without success. I reason it did not end, but I'm not sure why. I'm not sure until I get dressed, eat, greet my family, and walk out the door and into the circus. I see people. They are all on the tightrope. It now comes to me. The dream never did finish. I'm living it in real life. I'm living *a balancing act.* We are all living *a balancing act.*

END NOTES

[1] Commonwealth v John Smith; Massachusetts, Worcester SS, Superior Court, Criminal Action #: 89-2446-2447. Thanks to Larry S. O'Connor, Esq. and John F. Smith who both granted me permission to write about this case without restriction. (Chapter 1)

[2] MGL Chapter 147 Section 28 (dealing with "divulgence of information"): Any person who is or has been an employee of a licensee and any licensee who divulges to anyone other than to his employer or as his employer shall direct, except before an authorized tribunal, any information acquired by him during such employment in respect to any of the work to which he has been assigned by such employer, and any such employee who willfully makes a false report to his employer in respect to any such work, shall be punished by a fine of not more than five hundred dollars or by imprisonment for not more than one year, or both. (Chapter 2)

[3] Thanks to Peter L. Ettenberg, Esq. who granted permission to write about this case without restriction, except for names, dates, and places. (Chapter 2)

[4] Commonwealth v Deborah Reid; Massachusetts, Worcester SS, Superior Court, Criminal Action #: 90-0120-0122. Thanks to Larry S. O'Connor, Esq. who granted permission to write about this case without restriction. (Chapter 3)

[5] Anonymous (Chapter 4)

[6] Commonwealth v. Gail Blair; ; Massachusetts, Worcester SS, Superior Court, Criminal Action #: 89-0150. Thanks to Larry S. O'Connor, Esq. who granted permission to write about this case without restriction. (Chapter 4)

[7] Ruth Bositis was my 10th grade English teacher at West Boylston HS; Neil Brophy was my ethics professor and counselor at Worcester State College; Tony Volpe was a long time music teacher at Algonquin Regional HS and is the current chorus director of the Northborough Area Community Chorus of which I am a member in the tenor section. (Chapter 4)

[8] Benjamin Franklin of Philadelphia; 1706-1790. US founding father, statesman, writer, printer, inventor, and signer of the US Constitution and Declaration of Independence. (Chapter 5)

[9] We lost, but through no fault of Judge McCann. The Jury found negligence but not proximate cause which we'll never quite understand. I think the Judge was surprised by the decision, as was I. We caught each others eye after the verdict. I could tell he felt our misery. Some day I might ask him about it. (Chapter 9)

[10] Mahatma Gandhi (Mohandas Karamchand Gandhi) of India, 1869-1948. Philosopher; non violent leader; deep thinker; idealist; and hero. (Chapter 10)

[11] The Kellogg Company changed the name of Sugar Pops to Sugar Corn Pops and then to Corn Pops. I still love them like I did when I was a kid no matter what the name. (Chapter 12)

[12] Pete Townshend; *Won't Get Fooled Again*, 1971. (Chapter 12)

[13] NESC Committee: Herbert Simon; Kitty Hailey; Diane Cowan; Lawrence "Al" Cross; Jimmie Mesis; Lloyd Davis (Chapter 12)

[14] Susan Lajoie; Tricia Bonzey; Scott Robidoux; Jessica Civale; Jason Lajoie; Jessica Lajoie (Chapter 12).

[15] *The Holy Bible*: 1 Samuel 17 (Chapter 13)

[16] H. Ellis Armistead is the principal of H. Ellis Armistead & Associates, Inc. of Denver, CO. He specializes in criminal, civil, and commercial investigation. Ellis has an AA in Police Science, a BA in Political Science, and an MPA in Public Administration. He has been a professional investigator all his life. Ellis is a Certified Legal Investigator and a Certified Fraud Examiner. He is considered a qualified expert in death and homicide investigation. Ellis granted an interview and talked openly about the McVeigh case on March 15, 2005. (Chapter 13)

[17] Thanks to Peter L. Ettenberg, Esq. and H. Ellis Armistead, CLI, for granting me permission to write about these cases with few restrictions. (Chapter 13)

[18] Commonwealth v Eddie Morales; Massachusetts, Hampden SS, Superior Court, Criminal Action #: 00-0156. (Chapter 13)

[19] *Worcester Telegram & Gazette,* December 29, 1999 Article by Associated Press reporter Jeff Donn- Officer's daughter not angry. (Chapter 13)

[20] *Worcester Telegram & Gazette,* December 30, 1999 Article- Morales' court- appointed lawyer represented Mortell defendant. (Chapter 13)

[21] Email dated March 17, 2001 from Ettenberg to Lajoie. (Chapter 13)

[22] Email dated February 20, 2005 from Ettenberg to Lajoie. (Chapter 13)

[23] USA v Timothy McVeigh, et al Court: codce Case # 1:1996cr00068. (Chapter 13)

[24] USC Title 28, Part VI, Chapter 153, Section 2255 states a prisoner in custody under sentence of a court established by Act of Congress claiming the right to be released upon the ground that the sentence was imposed in violation of the Constitution or laws of the United States, or that the court was without jurisdiction to impose such sentence, or that the sentence was in excess of the maximum authorized by law, or is otherwise subject to collateral attack, may move the court which imposed the sentence to vacate, set aside or correct the sentence. (Chapter 13)

[25] Marc Twain is quoted to have said "Truth is stranger than fiction." (Chapter 14)

BIBLIOGRAPHY

Armistead, H. Ellis, Curriculum Vitae, 2005.

http://pacer.uspci.uscourts.gov; CODCE 1:1996cr00068; USA v. McVeigh et al.

http://homepage.mac.com/cparada/GML/Sisyphus.html

King, Stephen, *On Writing: Memoir of the Craft.* New York, Scribner, 2000.

Lajoie Investigations, Inc. case files; Eddie Morales; John Smith; Deborah Reid; Gail Blair and a number of other case files in which names were not mentioned.

Lincoln, Abraham, *Wisdom & Wit,* edited by Louise Bachelder. New York, Peter Pauper Press, Inc, 1965.

National Association of Legal Investigators, *Code of Ethics,* 1967.

Steers, Jr., Edward, *Blood On The Moon: The Assassination of Abraham Lincoln.* Kentucky, The University Press of Kentucky, 2001.

United States Code: Title 28; Part VI; Chapter 153; Section 2255. Federal custody; remedies on motion attacking sentence; www.findlaw.com.

www.CNN.com, 2001 law archives, McVeigh.

www.CNN.com, 2001 Specials

www.courttv.com, 2001 archives, McVeigh.

CREDITS & ACKNOWLEDGEMENTS

All chapter title page quotes were obtained from three sources as follows:

Beginning Quote: King, Stephen, *On Writing: Memoir of the Craft*. New York, Scribner, 2000, and can be found on page 69 of the Pocket Book printing.
Chapter 1-15 Quotes: Lincoln, Abraham, *Wisdom & Wit*, edited by Louise Bachelder. New York, Peter Pauper Press, Inc, 1965, and can be found within the pages of 5 thru 51.
End Quote: Billy Joel, song *Vienna* from The Stranger album, 1977.

I want to thank my parents, Raymond W. and Coralie A. Lajoie, for interviews they gave me in February and March of 2005 and for everything they have done for me and my family. I love you both. Interviews were also given by Lawrence S. O'Connor, Peter L. Ettenberg, and H. Ellis Armistead. I'm extremely grateful for their time and candor.

I extend much thanks and appreciation to award-winning author Michael Koryta (*Tonight I Said Goodbye,* Thomas Dunne Books, New York) for providing skilled advice and direction throughout the writing and publishing process. He is a superb, talented writer, and a good investigator, at 21 years. Wait until he's 51....I hope I'm alive to see it.

The staff at Lajoie Investigations, Inc. through the years deserves much appreciation, attention, respect, and admiration. Thank you all for opening my eyes. Special thanks to Tricia Bonzey (Bean) because I couldn't have done what I've done in my career without her daily aid, advice, and assistance. Heartfelt thanks to the current staff at LII for having to put up with me during this process: In addition to Trish, the rest are Jessica Civale, Kathryn Rudy, Scott Robidoux, Jason Lajoie, Matthew Fiedler, Jessica Lajoie, Kellie Yankauskas, and Susan Lajoie.

No doubt I couldn't have had a better Copy Editor in Tricia Bonzey. No one, and I do mean no one, types faster with more efficiency than Trish. And she's a great investigator to boot. Thank you from the bottom of my heart.

Mark Waitkus, John Gaston, and Anne Ashley are my experts in the area of artistic coordination, illustration, and cover design. And while the deadlines were tough, they came through in a big time way. Thanks!

Of course, it is without question that many, many thanks are due my loving wife, Susan, and three fabulous children, Jason, Jessica, and Jacqueline. Their patience, advice, love, and attention help me make it through each and every day. They inspire, encourage, and motivate me.

Special thanks to my In-Laws, Pete and Shirley Petterson, who do so much for Susan and I out of nothing but love without a complaint. There isn't a nicer human being on the face of the Earth than E.W. (Pete) Petterson. If I ever come back to the PI world in an afterlife, I want to come back as Pete Petterson.

I cannot forget the clients. This book would not exist but for the clients. I consider myself lucky to have clientele who believe in me. Thank you. I will never let you down.

APPENDIX

Lajoie Investigations Inc Business Plan, 1989

SUMMARY

THE COMPANY

Lajoie Investigations Inc. is a start up business that will provide investigative services to attorneys, insurance companies, corporate accounts, and the private sector.

THE MARKET

The total market in the present social environment is expanding at a phenomenal rate. From all indications the expansive growth will continue as the need for more detailed information concerning lifestyles and values grow in relation to:

- hiring of responsible employees

- increasing numbers of fraudulent insurance claims
- corporate accountability
- criminal investigations
- tort litigation
- domestic issues

PROFITABILITY

The profitability of Lajoie Investigations Inc. is based upon the following fundamental business principles:

- low start up cost
- low overhead
- client paid expenses
- minimal accounts receivables

DESCRIPTION OF THE BUSINESS

Lajoie Investigations Inc. is being formed to capitalize on the growing demand for quality investigative services. We will offer a full range of services to attorneys, insurance companies, corporations, and the private sector. Specifically, the agency will conduct Investigations in the following areas:

<u>Civil and criminal investigation for attorneys will be a large segment of the business</u>.
Investigation will be conducted in cases dealing with:

a.) tort liability
b.) rape
c.) assault
d.) homicide

Insurance investigation for claim departments will be another large segment of the business and will include:

a.) surveillance in bodily injury and workers compensation cases
b.) fraudulent property/casualty claims investigation
c.) coverage, liability, and damage claims investigation

Corporate investigation relevant to employees, competitors, and the reduction of shrink will focus on:

a.) potential employee background check
b.) asset verification
c.) corporate accountability and exercise of responsibility
d.) in house activity check while on the job

Domestic investigation will focus on:

a.) surveillance
b.) divorce and custody issues
c.) missing persons

STRUCTURE

The business will be incorporated under sub-chapter S. John M. Lajoie will be principal stockholder. The agency will be fully licensed and bonded under the regulations and statutes of the Commonwealth of Massachusetts. Liability risk will be minimized by implementing the above approach and obtaining proper insurances. This is a yearly, fully operational business that has no season. Daily and hourly operation will be sensitive to the demands of market and the specific case being investigated.

LOCATI ON

Lajoie Investigations Inc. will be located in its own office in downtown Worcester, Massachusetts. The business will primarily focus on Worcester and Worcester County, but will also include statewide investigation. This Worcester location strategically locates the agency and gives the company immediate accessibility to the major market, namely attorneys and insurance companies. It also is centrally located in relation to record keeping and research centers such as: City Hall, the county courthouse, and the police department. This business location will also give the agency credibility and visibility.

MARKET

In recent years current trends of the social and economic environment have facilitated the need and the growth of investigative services in legal, criminal, corporate, and domestic areas. Necessity and demand for accurate and detailed information in civil and criminal litigation creates a vast market serviced by very few qualified, professional, and licensed investigators.

Market research in Worcester and the Worcester county area has substantiated the following:

1. *Legal firms and independent attorneys* are realizing a much greater need for investigative services to prove claims before costly and time wasting court litigation ensues. Research has shown that this market prefers using a small local agency for their work because: it is cost efficient (large agency fees can be prohibitive).... the local agency is familiar with the area....small agency will be more detail oriented....attorneys prefer using an

agency that he/she can have immediate access to as the need arises.

2. *Insurance companies* in the area are a substantial segment of the market. A large part of private sector investigative personnel are recruited from the ranks of local and state law enforcement agencies and the FBI. This group of individuals, though highly skilled in specific areas, lacks the knowledge and background in tort liability and insurance investigation. National investigative firms are primarily focused on volume. The work is not as detailed and as comprehensive as required in some cases. Insurance companies are anxious to do business with a smaller firm for this reason. Generally speaking, local and regional claim centers for insurance companies develop long term working relationships with smaller investigating agencies, thus ensuring repeat business. Casualty claims have dramatically risen, creating a demand for detail oriented investigators to conduct surveillance of individuals to determine if there is a fraudulent injury. It is necessary to obtain and record statements concerning coverage, liability and damage issues on all lines insurance claim matters. These investigations require claims investigation knowledge and comprehension of insurance law. New tort reform laws dealing with motor vehicles and other insurance lines increase the need for qualified people, as well as accurate and knowledgeable procedures.

3. *Corporate sector investigation* will be will be an expanding market for the following reasons:

- Social environment has created a need for extensive and detailed background checks of potential employees hired into sensitive areas in business.

- Corporations find a need for in house investigation to minimize loss as a result of dishonest employees and drug activity.
- Surveillance of in house activities to eradicate drug use in the work place and identify dishonest employees.

4. *Private sector investigation* will be an increasing segment of the investigative market even though local customs and climate have not created a large demand for investigative services, except in the following areas:

- Surveillance to prove allegations made in a contested divorce suit.
- Fitness of a parent in a custody fight.
- Locating missing persons in probate cases and other matters.
- Fact finding in child support and alimony court actions.

COMPETITION

There are two local agencies that are noteworthy as competitors. They are small Investigative firms that have started as one man operations and have shown phenomenal growth in the last few years. Both firms cater to the insurance industry and attorneys. Both are passive businesses; none aggressively woos the market. The owners of these agencies have found the growth rate, without active marketing, to be staggering. Each of these businesses have turned clients away because of case overload in order to slow the growth rate of their company.

1. Info-Serve Inc.

Shrewsbury, MA 01545

Incorporated 1984....1 man operation start up 1989....3 man operation

Market....Insurance industry and attorneys

Marketing....no established program, relies on word of mouth

Growth rate....first three years doubled....voluntarily slowed growth rate to 20% in the 4th year

Fee schedule....$40 per hour plus expenses

Start up cost....12 to 15K (home base)

2. Poma-Wheeler Agency Inc.

East Longmeadow, MA. 01028

Incorporated 1983....one- man operation start up; 1989....growth to10-man operation Market....Insurance companies and attorneys....specializes in surveillance concerning disability claims; video and photo service; statements....background checks and asset checks.

Marketing....guerilla marketing techniques....high visibility in business community....cold calling.

Growth rate... 1st year gross....35 to 40K (net 23 to 24K)
2nd year gross....50 to 55K (net 40 to 45K)
3rd year gross....60 to 70K <net 50 to 55K)
1989....company's closing on a gross of 500K per year.

Fee schedule....$40 per hour plus expenses

Start up cost: under 50K (office outside home)

PROFITABILITY

Profitability of Lajoie Investigations Inc. is ensured by an ever expanding market. The credentials of the resident manager, John Lajoie, in the field of investigation are impeccable and his knowledge of the insurance claims industry is in-depth. By adhering to the following approach profit will be maximized.

- Awareness will be created by centrally locating for maximum visibility
- Direct mailings
- Trade publication advertising
- Tele Marketing
- Networking with and through present contacts
- Low overhead staff will consist of 2 part time clericals (no immediate benefits will be given)
- Fee schedule will be competitive
- Client will pay all expenses in addition to the hourly fee
- Account receivables will be minimized by instituting a policy of prepayment or partial advance payment.

As the industry continues to grow Lajoie Investigations Inc. will capture its share of the market and remain profitable by being extremely competitive, marketing aggressively, minimizing expenses, careful planning for continued growth and adjusting the business plan and goals as growth occurs.

[illegible] INVESTIGATIONS, INC.
PROJECTED STATEMENT OF OPERATIONS
For the Period 07/01/95 to 06/30/96

Rounded to Nearest $1

	Jul	Aug	Sep	Oct	Nov	Dec	Jan	Feb	Mar	Apr	May	Jun	[illegible]
Revenues	3,000	4,900	9,050	9,000	9,500	9,000	14,000	13,000	13,000	13,000	13,500	13,902	[illegible]
Operating Expenses	14,079	5,252	5,852	5,482	5,782	5,934	6,129	5,[illegible]70	9,470	2,[illegible]	8,172	8,170	[illegible]
Depreciation	183	185	183	183	183	183	183	183	183	183	183	183	
Net Income/(Loss) Before Interest and Taxes	($11,262)	2,725	3,103	3,531	3,535	1,255	5,447	5,447	5,447	5,447	5,157	5,447	[illegible]
Interest:													
Interest Expense	176	276	252	133	184	147	117	102	96	43	85	82	
Interest Income	0	0	0	0	0	0	0	0	0	0	0	0	
Net Income/(Loss) Before Taxes	(10,[illegible])	2,509	2,825	3,850	2,851	3,738	5,330	5,345	5,351	5,356	5,362	5,[illegible]	[illegible]
Provision for Income Tax	0	0	0	0	0	0	0	0	0	0	0	0	
Net Income/(Loss)	($14,000)	$2,459	$2,853	$2,826	$2,851	$2,738	$5,330	$5,345	$5,351	$5,356	$5,362	$5,367	[illegible]

LASER INVESTIGATIONS, INC.
Analysis of Projected Operating Expenses
For the Period 07/01/89 to 06/30/90

Rounded to Nearest $1

	Jul	Aug	Sep	Oct	Nov	Dec	Jan	Feb	Mar	Apr	May	Jun	Year
Salary - [illegible]	$2,125	$2,125	$2,125	$2,125	$2,125	$2,125	$2,125	$2,125	$2,125	$2,125	$2,125	$2,125	$25,
Secretary	250	1,023	1,327	1,342	1,342	1,342	1,342	1,342	1,342	1,342	1,342	1,342	14,
Investigator	0	0	0	0	0	0	2,000	2,000	2,000	2,000	2,000	2,000	12,
Invest. asst.	0	400	400	400	400	400	400	400	400	400	400	400	4,
Payroll taxes	312	373	372	392	392	496	511	516	516	616	516	516	5,
Business insurance	42	50	50	52	52	54	82	82	42	82	82	82	
Advertising	150	131	120	120	120	120	120	120	120	120	120	120	1,
Incorp. costs	100	0	0	0	0	0	0	0	0	0	0	0	
Insurance - liability	1,000	0	0	0	0	0	0	0	0	0	0	0	1,
Telephone	600	300	300	300	300	300	300	300	300	300	300	300	3,
Office supplies	500	250	250	250	250	200	250	250	200	200	200	200	2
Fees	500	75	75	75	75	75	75	75	75	75	75	75	1
Office [illegible]	50	50	50	50	50	50	50	50	50	50	50	50	
Rental [illegible]	1,500	400	200	100	100	100	100	500	100	100	100	100	3
Bank	100	0	0	0	0	0	0	0	0	0	0	0	
Vehicle	1,100	0	0	0	0	0	0	0	0	0	0	0	1
Occupancy costs	550	550	550	550	550	550	550	550	550	550	550	550	6
Miscellaneous	300	200	200	200	200	200	200	200	200	200	200	200	2
Total	$11,611	$5,932	$5,622	$5,782	$5,782	$5,922	$8,176	$8,116	$8,176	$8,176	$8,176	$8,176	$81

"VIENNA WAITS FOR YOU"

Billy Joel

ABOUT THE AUTHOR

John M. Lajoie is known throughout the country for his skill and experience as a private investigator, and for his dedication to the field of professional private investigation. Lajoie has turned the one-man operation he began in 1989 into one of the largest investigative firms in central Massachusetts. John is a Certified Legal Investigator, a Certified Criminal Defense Investigator, a Certified International Investigator, and a Board Certified Professional Investigator. His case experience has ranged from high-profile homicides to simple auto accidents, and his client base from the rich and famous to the homeless and indigent. He is a member of many national and international professional investigator organizations, and is frequently recognized by these groups for his outstanding work and contributions to the investigative profession and the community. Lajoie was born and raised in Worcester, Massachusetts and now lives in Sterling with his wife, Susan, and three children. For more information on Mr. Lajoie visit his website at www.PrivateInvestigator.com.

Printed in the United States
34446LVS00001B/58-261

9 781420 869392